HOPE
AND
GLORY

EPIC STORIES
OF EMPIRE AND
COMMONWEALTH

Melissa Blackburn is Associate Producer of *Hope and Glory*, and principal author of this accompanying book. Nick Maddocks is Producer/Director of *Hope and Glory* and has worked on a number of series for the BBC, ITV1 and C4. Clair Titley is an award-winning graduate of UWE, and *Hope and Glory*'s researcher. Steve Humphries is Series Editor. He is the author of over twenty social history books documenting life in twentieth-century Britain, many of them written to accompany television series, including *A Secret World of Sex*, *The Call of the Sea* and *Green and Pleasant Land*. He set up the independent TV production company Testimony Films in Bristol in 1992.

HOPE
AND
GLORY

EPIC STORIES
OF EMPIRE AND
COMMONWEALTH

MELISSA BLACKBURN, STEVE HUMPHRIES,
NICK MADDOCKS AND CLAIR TITLEY

SUTTON PUBLISHING
ITV1 AND TESTIMONY FILMS

First published in the United Kingdom in 2004 by
Sutton Publishing Limited · Phoenix Mill
Thrupp · Stroud · Gloucestershire · GL5 2BU
in association with ITV1

This book is based upon the ITV1 West of England television series
produced by Testimony Films.

British Library Cataloguing in Publication Data
A catalogue record for this book is available from the British Library.

ISBN 0-7509-3540-5

Typeset in 11.5/15pt Garamond
Typesetting and origination by
Sutton Publishing Limited.
Printed and bound in England by
J.H. Haynes & Co. Ltd, Sparkford.

Dedicated with love to
Barbara and Robert Blackburn

Contents

Acknowledgements

Special thanks to James Garrett at HTV, for believing in the project and supporting it. Thanks also to Ifty Khan and Margaret Whitcombe at HTV for their expertise and advice. We are also grateful to Gareth Griffiths, Mary Ingoldby, Ben Woodhams, Faisal Khalif, Jan Vaughan and Jo Hopkins at the British Empire and Commonwealth Museum for all their help and insight.

We would like to thank the contributors to this book for sharing their experiences and for their time and endless patience: Rosalind Balcon, Sheila Mitchell Bane, Ben Bousquet, Mohindra Chowdhry, Alan Chidgey, Roy Hackett, Alice Harper, John Hennessey, Hazel Hooper, Rosa Hui, Norman Jones, Precious McKenzie, Alok and Priti Ray and Sadie Regan.

Thank you to Richard Clutterbuck, Jill and Ivor Maddocks, Madge Dresser, Cluna Donnelly and the Malcolm X Centre's Elders' Forum, the Bristol Record Office, Joe Short and especially Matt Coster.

Finally, thank you to all at Sutton Publishing, from all of us.

Hazel Hooper in December 1926.

ONE

MEMORIES OF EMPIRE

This book uses living memory to explore the close links between the south-west of England and the British Empire and Commonwealth in the twentieth century. Incredibly, at its height between the world wars, Britain ruled a quarter of the globe and 600 million people. But while its size and power still inspire awe, many people see the heyday of empire as a deeply shameful period: Britain's massive complicity in the slave trade, its economic exploitation of its subjects, its bloody enforcement of British rule and its practices of racial discrimination and segregation are appalling to us today. However, others point to a more beneficial legacy, to an empire that hungered for trade but that also spread liberty, prosperity and the English language around the world. What is not in doubt is that the British Empire was the biggest empire the world has ever seen, and it shaped the world we live in today more than anything else in the last 500 years. Documenting its history is vital to our understanding of our present and our future, and this was the inspiration for *Hope and Glory* and the six-part television series it accompanies.

The original idea for this project came from a display we made for the recently opened British Empire and Commonwealth Museum in Bristol, whose twenty permanent galleries span 500 years of the history of the British Empire, from its rise through trade and colonisation, to the height of British rule in the Victorian and Edwardian eras, to its final demise. In the last gallery, the museum planned to use its huge oral history archive as the basis for a video display that would allow people whose lives were shaped by the empire and commonwealth to tell their stories. For the museum, oral history opened up the past in a way that facts and figures could not: it could help to unravel the complicated history of the British Empire by giving people the freedom to tell their stories their way and so create a more human picture of history. They hoped that this kind of first-person, eyewitness testimony would give a voice to those hidden from history: ethnic minorities, impoverished migrants and refugees and the women of empire, offering a more complete and vivid picture of the rise and fall of the British Empire in the twentieth century.

In a series of dramatic personal journeys, those who went out to live in the old empire are captured on film telling their stories alongside those who came to Britain from the former colonies. The video display features people from all over Britain, among them Ben Bousquet, a West Indian elder who speaks passionately about his experience of migration to England:

> I'm from St Lucia. I came to this country when I was sixteen years old in 1956. I was often humiliated by people stopping me, and asking me if I had a tail. They wanted to touch my tail. They wanted to rub my skin on Christmas Day. They thought that would bring them luck in the coming year. They knew nothing about us and about the Commonwealth and what it was meant to be all about. We knew more about the English than the English did.

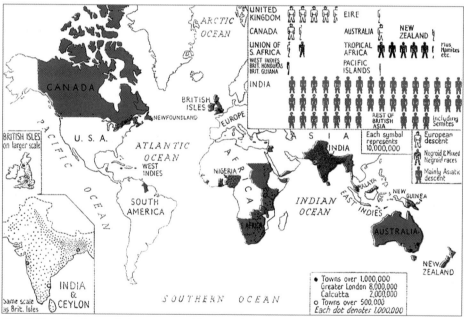

The British Empire and Commonwealth, seen here in 1944, was the biggest empire the world has ever seen, reaching its height in the 1920s and 1930s. It covered 25 per cent of the globe, colouring every schoolchild's map a dark pink; it stretched out across the dominions of Australia, Canada, New Zealand and South Africa; it included large parts of southern and western Africa, as well as the old slave-trading colonies on the east coast; and it engulfed the huge Indian subcontinent and parts of South East Asia including Malaya and Hong Kong and the islands of the West Indies. In all, between the two world wars, the population of Britain's Empire and Commonwealth numbered six hundred million. Even today, the Commonwealth's fifty-four ex-colonies, with the Queen as their nominal head of state, make up a quarter of the world's population.

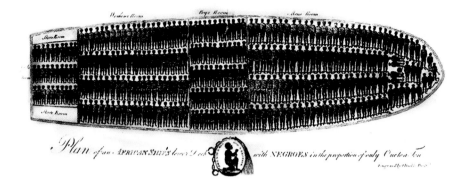

THE above Plate represents the lower deck of an African Ship of 297 tons burthen, with the Slaves stowed on it, in the proportion of not quite one to a ton.

In the Men's apartment, the space allowed to each is six feet in length, by sixteen inches in breadth.—The Boys are each allowed five feet by fourteen inches.—The Women, five feet ten inches, by fixteen inches; and the Girls, four feet by one foot each.—The perpendicular height between the Decks, is five feet eight inches.

The Men are fastened together two and two, by handcuffs on their wrists, and by irons rivetted on their legs.—They are brought up on the main deck every day, about eight o'clock, and as each pair ascend, a strong chain, fastened by ring-bolts to the deck, is passed through their Shackles; a precaution absolutely necessary to prevent insurrections.—In this state, if the weather is favourable, they are permitted to remain about one-third part of the twenty four hours, and during this interval they are fed, and their apartment below is cleaned; but when the weather is bad, even these indulgences cannot be granted them, and they are only permitted to come up in small companies, of about ten at a time, to be fed, where after remaining a quarter of an hour, each mess is obliged to give place to the next in rotation.

It may perhaps be conceived, from the crouded state in which the Slaves appear in the Plate, that an unusual and exaggerated instance has been produced; this, however, is so far from being the case, that no ship, if her intended cargo can be procured, ever carries a less number than one to a ton, and the usual practice has been to carry nearly double that number: The Bill which was passed during the last Session of Parliament, only restricts the carriage, to five Slaves for three tons; and the Brooks, of Liverpool, a capital ship; from which the above sketch was proportioned, did, in one voyage, actually carry 609 Slaves, which is more than double the number that appear in the plate.——The mode of stowing them was as follows:—Platforms, or wide shelves were erected, between the decks, extending so far from the sides towards the middle of the vessel, as to be capable of containing four additional rows of Slaves, by which means the perpendicular height between each tier, after allowing for the beams and platforms, was reduced to two feet six inches; so that they could not even sit in an erect posture; besides which, in the Men's apartment, instead of four rows, five were stowed, by placing the heads of one between the thighs of another.—All the horrors of this situation are still multiplied in the smaller vessels.—The Kitty, of 137 tons, had only one foot ten inches, and the Venus, of 146 tons, only one foot nine inches perpendicular height above each layer.

The above mode of carrying the Slaves, however, is only one, among a thousand other miseries, which those unhappy and devoted creatures suffer from this disgraceful Traffick of the Human Species; which in every part of its progress, exhibits scenes that strike us with horror and indignation.—If we regard the first stage of it on the Continent of Africa, we find that a hundred thousand Slaves are annually produced there for exportation, the greatest part of whom consists of innocent persons, torn from their dearest friends and connections, sometimes by force, and sometimes by treachery. Of these, experience has shewn, that five and forty thousand perish, either in the dreadful mode of conveyance before described, or within two years after their arrival at the plantations, before they are seasoned to the climate.—Those who unhappily survive these hardships, are destined like beasts of burthen, to exhaust their lives in the unremitting labours of a Slavery, without recompence, and without hope.

The Inhumanity of this Trade, indeed, is so notorious, and so universally admitted, that even the advocates for the continuance of it, have rested all their arguments on the political inexpediency of its abolition; and in order to strengthen a weak cause, have either maliciously or ignorantly confounded together the emancipation of the negroes already in Slavery, with the abolition of the Trade; and thus many well-meaning people have become enemies to the cause, by the apprehensions that private property will be materially injured by the success of it.—To such, it becomes a necessary information, that liberating the Slaves forms no part of the present system; and so far will the prohibition of a future trade be from injuring private property, that the value of every Slave will be very considerably increased, from the moment that event takes place, and a more kind and tender treatment will immediately be insured to them by their Masters, from the necessity every Planter will then be under to keep up his stock, by natural means; a practice which some humane inhabitants of the Islands have pursued with the greatest success, and upon whose estates no new Negroes have been purchased for a number of years, the death vacancies having been supplied by young ones, born and bred in their own Plantations.—Thus then the value of private property will not only suffer no diminution, but will be very considerably inhanced by the abolition of the Trade.—It now only remains to see how the Public and the Slave Merchants will be affected by it.

It is said by the well-wishers to this Trade, that the suppression of it will destroy a great nursery for seamen, and annihilate a very considerable source of commercial profit. In answer to these objections, Mr. Clarkson, in his admirable treatise on the impolicy of the Trade, lays down two positions, which he has proved from the most incontestible authority.—First, that so far from being a Nursery, it has been constantly and regularly a Grave for our Seamen; for that in this Traffick only, more Men perish in ONE Year, than in all the other Trades of Great-Britain, in TWO Years: And, secondly, that the balance of the trade, from its extreme precariousness and uncertainty, is so notoriously against the Merchants, that if all the vessels, employed in it were the property of one Man, he would infallibly, at the end of their voyages, find himself a loser.

As then the Cruelty and Inhumanity of this Trade must be universally admitted and lamented, and as the policy or impolicy of its abolition is a question which the wisdom of the Legislature must ultimately decide upon, and which it can only be enabled to form a just estimate of, by the most thorough investigation of all its relations and dependencies; it becomes the indispensible duty of every friend to humanity, however his speculations may have led him to conclude on the political tendency of the measure, to stand forward, and to assist the Committees, either by producing such facts as he may himself be acquainted with, or by subscribing, to enable them to procure and transmit to the Legislature, such evidence as will tend to throw the necessary lights on the subject.—And people would do well to consider that it does not often fall to the lot of individuals, to have an opportunity of performing so important a moral and religious duty, as that of endeavouring to put an end to a practice, which may, without exaggeration, be stiled one of the greatest evils at this day existing upon the earth.

By the Plymouth Committee,

W. Elford, Chairman.

A plan of a slave ship. Between 1685 and 1807 about 2.8 million slaves were taken from Africa by British slave-traders, with Bristol taking a fifth of these. Over 2,000 'slaver ships' made voyages from Bristol's docks during this time. There was little slave trading in Bristol, because slaves were mostly sold in the Caribbean and America, and in fact by 1772 it was illegal to force slaves to be taken from the UK. But the practice continued, with the writer Hannah More witnessing the seizure in Bristol of a black woman who had run away because she did not want to return to the West Indies: 'The public crier offered a guinea to any one who hunted her down, and at length the poor trembling wretch was dragged out from a hole in the top of a house, where she had hid herself, and forced onboard ship.'

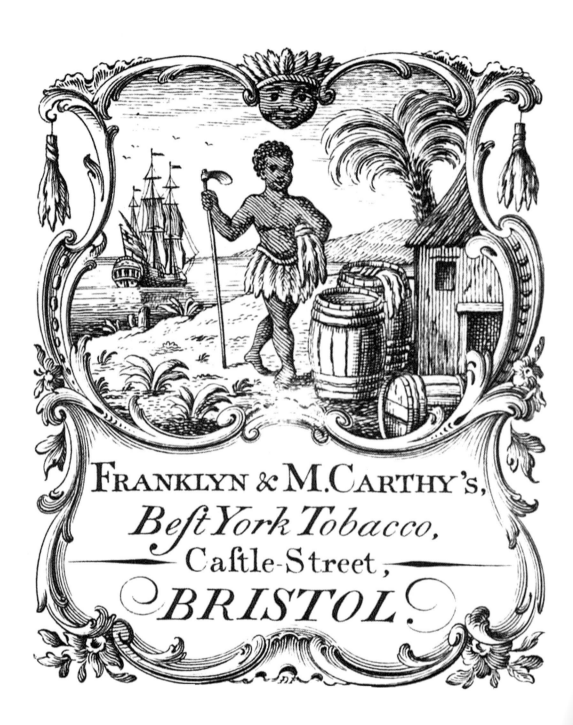

FRANKLYN & M.CARTHY's,
Beſt York Tobacco,
Caſtle-Street,
BRISTOL.

Tobacco was part of Bristol's economy until comparatively recently. It came from the colonies of Maryland and Virginia, and by the end of the seventeenth century Bristol was handling millions of pounds in weight of tobacco. Advertisements like this were common, depicting the children of black slaves who laboured on the plantations.

Mr Chowdhry, a Sikh resplendent in a colourful turban who came to Bristol from India, describes falling from a crane 100 feet up into the Avonmouth docks where he worked: 'I had a dip and it drenched my turban!' Miraculously he wasn't hurt. 'Coming to England was a fantastic journey for me; I'm glad I came.'

The display has been popular with the public, but we felt we had only touched the surface of a deeply complex and captivating history, and that there were many more stories to tell. We wanted to concentrate purely on those with links to the south-west, broadly defined as Bristol, Somerset, South Gloucestershire and Wiltshire. The south-west has strong links with the British Empire, especially through the trading port of Bristol and the large numbers of locals who left to live, work or fight in the old colonies. Similarly, the area is home to strong communities from Asia, the Caribbean and Africa, who arrived here as a direct result of the colonial experience. Because the history of the empire and commonwealth is so vast, the south-west gives valuable focus to a potentially unwieldy subject. Research for this new project began in the autumn of 2002, continuing through 2003. We contacted many local community groups, placed newspaper advertisements calling for people's memories and sent countless letters and emails. We spoke to hundreds of men and women who told us their stories.

It became clear that many of their stories had an epic theme in common, one of the great themes of empire: the constant movement of peoples. This was no surprise. The rise of the British Empire and Commonwealth created the biggest mass migration in human history: between the early 1600s and the 1950s, more than twenty million people left Britain for the lands of empire. Some left in search of riches or power, others in search of religious or political freedom. Some were transported as criminals or indentured servants. Others were civil servants, engineers, soldiers, foresters or missionaries. Then again, since the 1950s more than a million people have come to Britain from the empire and commonwealth to live and work here as citizens, creating a new country where 300 languages are spoken and fourteen faiths practised. The south-west itself has been the scene of endless comings and goings, a gateway of empire for 500 years. While this book concentrates on its twentieth-century oral history, it is helpful to understand some of the forces of empire that shaped the south-west, and that affected the lives of so many of today's locals.[1]

Five hundred years ago the city of Bristol was as central to the region as it is today. Clustered round the rivers Avon and Frome as they snake out into the huge estuary of the Severn, Bristol's thriving port was in the centre of the city, where the tall ships seemed to sail through the streets, their sails and long masts

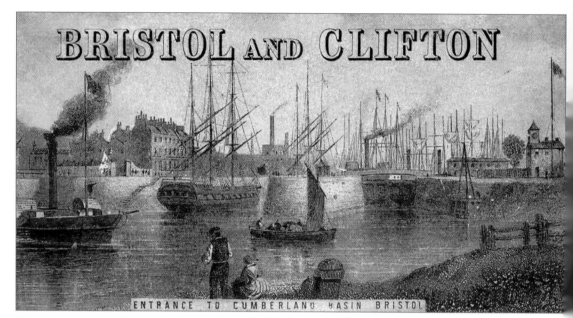

The placement of Bristol port in the centre of the city and its tidal nature meant that it was often difficult for ships to navigate. With the invention of steamships new docks had to be built out at Avonmouth to handle the endless goods of empire that poured into Bristol.

glimpsed through the narrow alleyways. John Cabot's epic 1497 voyage of discovery to Newfoundland lit a fire in every Bristol merchant's heart, and from then on the city was powered by trade with the New World. It would have been a noisy, bustling place, its ships heading out to the plantations of the newly claimed colonies of Virginia, Barbados and Jamaica, carrying British goods and plantation workers – the very first emigrants of empire. However, the burgeoning British appetite for new luxuries such as sugar, tobacco and rum soon created a corresponding thirst for manpower on the plantations. Although ten thousand Bristolians had emigrated by the end of the seventeenth century, many as transportees, white slaves or indentured servants, by 1650 the public mood had turned against emigration, many feeling that it was weakening the country. This feeling was to last until about 1800, possibly because of rumours of the deadly heat, disease and primitive conditions in the plantations. Fresh manpower needed to be found, and, when the London-based Royal African Company's monopoly on the British slave trade ended, Bristol merchants saw their chance.

Bristol's slave-trading past is infamous: it was soon the second most powerful slave-trader after London, and there is no doubt that the prosperity of the entire south-west region was built on the lives of the half a million African slaves who were bought and sold by Bristol's ships in the eighteenth century.[2] Eventually Bristol's share of the trade began to dwindle, but such was the city's involvement in the trade that, when Wilberforce's first Abolition of Slavery bill was defeated in the Commons, there were fireworks and cannons fired on Brandon Hill and church bells were rung across Bristol. But domestic pressure and increasing revolts on the plantations made abolition in 1807 almost inevitable, by which time Bristol's direct part in the trade had declined to almost nothing. However, the imperial movement of people of which slavery was a part meant that there was a small black community in Bristol from the mid-seventeenth century, made up of black servants, slaves and nannies brought back by wealthy plantation-owners, Indian lascar sailors and black seamen and merchants.[3]

After Waterloo in 1815, Britain was established as one of the great world powers, with complete naval supremacy. Gradually the British dislike of

ll ships such as these resting in Calcutta's docks around 1880 were the lifeblood of the British Empire. There e records of small Asian communities in Gloucestershire and Bristol from the eighteenth century, some of 1om were lascars or merchant seaman and some of whom came to England to study law or medicine. though most of Bristol's trade was with America and the Caribbean, Bristol's imperial links with India came much stronger in the nineteenth century.

The classic image of empire, such as this early photograph of the Raja of Suket in 1919, is of the pomp and circumstance of British India, the jewel in the crown of empire. Less than thirty years after this photograph was taken, India gained its independence and the British Empire began to topple.

emigration melted away, and was replaced with a new, Victorian obsession: the expansion of what was now called the British Empire. Hundreds of thousands flocked abroad, the *Plymouth Times* in January 1848 claiming that there were 'forty single ladies for every single man in Weston-super-Mare', as men left for work abroad in their droves. Although Bristolians were among the first convicts to be transported to Australia in 1787, by the 1840s the government was encouraging working-class emigration, and people from the south-west flocked to Australia, New Zealand and Canada. Fifteen thousand alone were taken from Bristol to Australia by the SS *Great Britain* in 1843. But again, not everyone went voluntarily. The Bristol Guardians sent batches of Bristol orphans over to Canada in the 1870s in order to buttress the population there. About 150 orphans were sent over a period of three years, and even back then there was a public outcry and the practice was stopped.[4]

By now Bristol's skyline was crammed with glassworks whose cones were ninety feet high and soap-makers using the plentiful waters of the Avon. There were lead-smelters and brass works, giant sugar refineries and tobacco factories. The advent of steamships in the first half of the nineteenth century and the opening of Bristol's new docks at Avonmouth brought yet more imperial trade to the city, and, after the monopoly of the East India Company had been broken, trade between Bristol and India began to flourish. Whilst thousands of Britons flocked to British India every year, there was a tiny trickle of Indians coming to the UK, most coming to attend British universities to study law or medicine. Rammohun Roy, often called the Father of India for his gentle and progressive nationalism, was one of the first Hindu Brahmin intellectuals to visit Bristol in 1833, and local ladies were apparently very taken with the tall, swarthy aristocrat. Sadly, after a sudden but short illness, he died and is buried at Arnos Vale cemetery. His death stimulated the social reformer Mary Carpenter to set up the National Indian Association to promote knowledge about India and understanding between Britons and Indians.

e Gold Coast had provided the slave ships with their grisly cargo, and it continued to provide Britain with e luxuries it craved. Here bananas are sold at a market in Ghana in the 1930s.

These lions were killed because they had been preying on local cattle in Kenya in the 1930s. The photo is by the writer and photographer Elspeth Huxley, who wrote a great deal about the British experience in Africa before the war.

By the turn of the century the might of the British Empire seemed unstoppable. The Great Coronation Durbar of 1903 celebrated Edward VII's succession in New Delhi, and in 1904 the first Empire Day was celebrated on 24 May throughout the land and in every British colony. After the victory of the First World War, in which Britain was supported by nearly two million imperial soldiers, the British Empire was swollen with gains from the defeated German and Turkish empires. But, just as the empire reached its peak, cracks began to appear. Britain had already given Dominion status to Australia (1901), New Zealand (1907) and South Africa (1909), meaning that, although the king was still sovereign, national parliaments had the independence to govern themselves. These cracks were widened by local movements like Mahatma Gandhi's increasingly popular passive resistance movement, which called for independence for India.

Nevertheless, the British Empire enjoyed its final heyday in the 1920s and 1930s, recent enough to be remembered by many people alive today. As the south-west began to recover from the Great War, the British flocked to the newly expanded empire, many in an effort to find peace after the horrors of the battlefield.

It was at this time that many of the people whose stories we feature in this book were born, Rosalind Balcon included. Rosalind's father decided to emigrate to Kenya, partly because he was concerned that another war might be on the horizon, and she remembers the shock that she felt having to leave England: 'It was pretty traumatic leaving because everyone had to say goodbye and we went down to the docks on a really miserable November day. But it was exciting too because we'd never been on a big ship before. We went on what we thought was the biggest ship in the world. I think it was 11,000 tonnes, which is now considered rather titchy.'

Hazel Hooper and her twin were born in England in 1922. Their parents took them back to India when they were six months old. 'I suppose it was a way of life which I absolutely loved. In fact I suppose I loved India more than anywhere because I knew it better than anywhere. So perhaps it meant home, perhaps I didn't realise we were the rulers. We'd never use that word, it's only in history I've heard that word.'

However, for many people in India, the British were very much the rulers, and the growing disquiet even manifested itself in the south-west: throughout the 1930s Dr Sukhsagar Datta and his colleagues in the Bristol Labour Party were campaigning vociferously for Indian freedom. As Gandhi's non-violent revolution gained pace, it was clear that British India's days were numbered. The Second World War erupted, drawing in two million troops from the colonies and tens of thousands of soldiers from the south-west. The war was the death knell of empire, and by the end of it a weakened Britain was forced to admit America's new supremacy and to give in to fresh and fervent demands for independence from its colonies. By 1947 India had gained independence and the country was split into Hindu and Muslim states, and the attempt to move millions of Muslims and Hindus to their newly allotted lands resulted in massive bloodshed. Priti Ray grew up in India but now lives in Bristol:

I was born in 1936 and grew up in West Bengal. The village I grew up in was self-sufficient and very progressive: it was almost completely Muslim, and we were Hindus, yet we grew up like a brother and sister. My father was a Gandhi supporter, and my grandma used to do the weaving and make all our

Rosalind Balcon and her twin sister, with father and grandfather in the West Country in the 1920s. Rosalind's father foresaw the coming Second World War, and felt that the family would be safer in Kenya. They emigrated in 1935.

saris and everything at home – we just boycotted all the British products. During the worst part of partition, we got all the women and children into our house and they stayed away from any trouble. And when the trouble was over after eleven days they went back. But it was a terrible time: so many people were chopped up. It was horrible.

For colonials like Hazel Hooper, who was later to settle in Bristol, it was devastating to be forced to leave India, but she was comforted by the belief that England's influence had been beneficial: 'We had left India a good legacy, because the universities and the schools were started or begun by English people. The hospitals, the railways system, which they say is about the best in the world. Although it's not run by Englishmen, we began it. And also, the English language, which they all learnt, all over India, and now that means Indians can go all over the world.' She became one of millions heading back to England as empire disintegrated, to a country that was very different from the one she'd been born in, to start a new life.

Still, people continued to emigrate, willingly or unwillingly. John Hennessey, who grew up in an orphanage in Bristol, was one of tens of thousands of

zel Hooper as a baby with her twin sister and elder brother, with their Indian servants at their house in dras, 1923.

These 'orphans' are on a train bound for Southampton, from where they'll be transported to Australia. Ov
150,000 orphans were sent out to Australia, Canada, Zimbabwe and South Africa to boost the whi
population – but, unbeknown to them, many had parents still living in Britain.

'orphans' who were sent out to Australia, Canada and South Africa in the 1940s, 1950s and 1960s. Although public anger had temporarily stopped the practice in Bristol in the 1870s, it continued into the twentieth century and emerged with renewed energy after the Second World War. The aim was to bolster the white populations of the colonies. As the Archbishop of Perth, Australia, said to the young boys and girls arriving on ships from Britain in 1938: 'At a time when empty cradles are contributing woefully to empty spaces, it is necessary to look for external sources of supply. And if we do not supply from our own stock, we are leaving ourselves all the more exposed to the menace of the teeming millions of our neighbouring Asiatic Races.' The Australian government asked its British counterpart to send out more British children to increase the white population. The call went out to churches and their agencies, with the Catholic Church being a particularly enthusiastic supporter of the initiative. The falsification of birth certificates and emigration documents was common, and the children were told that they had no living relatives left in Britain and that Australia was now their home. But this was often a lie. Most of the children were not orphans, but had been removed from their parents illegally: 87 per cent of all children from Catholic agencies came to Australia without the consent of their parents, and 96 per cent of those sent had one or both parents alive. The practice stopped in the late 1960s when they simply ran out of children to send, and it was decades later that the harsh conditions and abuse that many of the children had experienced were exposed.

At the same time as the orphans were shipped off to an uncertain future, Britons were being encouraged to emigrate to Australia as part of the 'Ten Pound Pom' scheme. It offered a cheap (£10) boat fare to Australia in the hope, again, of building up the country's white population, and for many south-west families it was a sunny, over-the-rainbow dream.

For newly divorced Sadie Regan, living in a terraced house in Avonmouth with her new husband Johnny, the scheme offered a fresh start away from the prejudice that divorced women then faced. By 1965 the couple were living near Brisbane with their three children: 'We were allocated a hut on an ex-military barracks, with the most basic of furnishing requirements. We met lots of friendly people from the UK, but not everything was wonderful of course. Mosquito nets were an essential protection from the ever-present mosquitoes, which loved to feast on the blood of freshly arrived Europeans!' Eventually they bought a house. 'It was a beautiful house with a yard like the Garden of Eden – banana trees, choco trees, figs. But when it was time to cut down the huge bunches of bananas, my husband got a shock. Tarantulas came out of every hand of fruit – first the parents, an enormous female the size of a mouse, and then millions of young ones! I had to hose him down and force them off him.'

For many Ten Pound Poms, however, leaving Britain meant not just the promise of a new life, but the pain of being parted from family and friends, possibly forever. 'One day, I got a call from my sister telling me our dad had died,' recalls Sadie. 'I was very sad, because I had adored my parents, particularly since they adopted me when I was six weeks old. I prayed hard that he and Mum were resting together.' When her husband's stepfather died a few years later, he began to worry about how his mother was coping back in

Sadie Regan with her husband, before they emigrated to Australia.

England. After six years of adventure, hardship and sunshine, the family decided to come home.

As empire fell apart in the 1950s and 1960s, the south-west experienced new waves of emigration and immigration. While the foot soldiers of the British Empire – its bureaucrats, officers and managers – came home from India, and new independence movements gathered pace in Africa and the Caribbean, the British government was calling out to the colonies to come and help rebuild war-torn Britain. There had been a very small black population in Bristol for hundreds of years, but in the 1950s government-sponsored Caribbean workers, some of whose ancestors were the African slaves who had helped build Bristol's prosperity, began creating a strong black community for the first time. For many, their first experience of the motherland was disappointing. The cities of the south-west – Bristol, Gloucester, Bath – had been badly bombed and first impressions were of poverty and dilapidation. It was often in the most run-down areas of the city, like St Paul's in Bristol, that the new arrivals were forced to make their homes. The cold, too, bothered many. But the racism and segregation that had often characterized the colonial experience, and that had arguably begun with the switch to black slavery, were a shock to these sons of empire, who considered themselves British and who were here to help rebuild the south-west. The experience of Roy Hackett was typical.

Man walking through St Paul's, 1960s. Although encouraged by the British government, who were desperate for help in rebuilding war-torn Britain, many Caribbean immigrants encountered a disappointingly cold and unwelcoming reception.

A man putting out a flag in St Paul's, 1960s.

Alok and Priti Ray around the time they first came to England in the early 1970s.

It was a very raw reception. It was not very friendly. It was not a welcoming one. . . . I had lived in Jamaica all the time amongst white people and I never thought that I was any different from them. When I came here I did see the difference. Because I was put in my place that I was black, that I was a nigger, and it made me very ashamed of even being British, actually.

But the black communities in the south-west, particularly in Bristol and Gloucester, and the increasing arrivals from India, Pakistan and later Bangladesh, were a legacy of empire that was here to stay. When Priti Ray arrived in England, Enoch Powell was planning his rivers-of-blood speech and the West Indian community in Bristol was creating the first St Paul's Festival in 1968, a celebration of an Afro-Caribbean culture that had once felt itself to be part of the motherland, but that was now, with Caribbean independence, able to stand on its own.

The instability and war resulting from the gradual transition to independence and democracy meant that south-west soldiers and national servicemen were sent out to places like Malaya, Suez, Cyprus and Kenya. The Malayan Emergency, which began in 1948, saw British rubber-planters, miners and

Priti Ray at home in Bristol.

Thousands of people from the south-west fought in the many post-war conflicts that resulted in the fall of the British Empire. Norman Jones (bottom) and his army friends were only eighteen when they were called up for National Service in 1953. 'They told us we'd be going to Malaya, and we was worried about it, 'cause we knew people had been killed over there, and there was a little bit of action over there.'

colonials attacked by Communist insurgents keen to take over the colony and oust the British. Norman Jones, from Bridgwater, was sent out in 1953 and found the experience disturbing:

Sometimes we went on patrol for two weeks, go through the rubber plantations into the jungle. These bandits used to terrorise the people who worked on the rubber trees and that. We used to have to go and try to catch 'em and try to find 'em. One morning we were on patrol, just a small platoon, about twelve of us. And these two bandits passed right in front of us, one of them is only ten yards away from me. My sergeant shot first because he was in charge, and killed a bandit, and I shot the other one and he was wounded. He ran back into the jungle. It ain't very nice.

vas the job of British soldiers in Malaya to find Communist insurgents who were attacking rubber-planters
miners. But the jungle was an unfamiliar environment, and for young recruits it was a gruelling
perience: 'We didn't wanna be there, not really, but we went along with it. You know, we was British, and
were soldiers and that's what we had to do. All the chaps and that, I mean, we all work together very
l. We had a bit of fun together and we had some hard times together as well.'

Like many of his colleagues, he was out there on National Service, and was only eighteen. 'Sometimes we had to go in the night, about ten o'clock at night, and go to a village, get them out of their beds, and get in the village and search it. It was unpleasant, but just something we had to do. Some of the lads used to go, "Let's have a bit of action!", and all that, and some of the boys did that. But I was the other way round. I wasn't gonna be a John Wayne, I wanted to go quietly. I didn't wanna die.'

The fall-out from the end of empire can be seen in the great diversity of the population in the south-west. While the British continued to emigrate, Asians who were expelled from Kenya and Uganda in the early 1970s began to arrive. After the Turkish invasion of Cyprus, an island so beautiful it was known as the 'Cinderella of the empire', more Greek-Cypriots arrived to join the existing Greek communities in Bristol and Weston-super-Mare. Unrest brought refugees

When British troops like Norman Jones (foreground) were on patrol, they had to sleep in the jungle: 'We'd tr all day, cutting through the jungle and all that, and then eventually about four o'clock in the afternoon you reach your place where you decided to camp. As it got dark, you could hear thousands of animals making noise. Really. A really loud noise. But after a while, a couple of hours, it would all go dead quiet. It w something, I must admit.'

from South Africa, Somalia and Zimbabwe, and thousands of people from all over the Commonwealth have come to the area to work and study. Nowadays there are thriving multicultural communities all over the south-west, with Bristol home to 4,500 of Asian descent, and 5,500 of Afro-Caribbean descent.

Today the British Empire is gone, but its history and its legacy are visible all over the south-west, from the tobacco factories and sugar refineries that still dot the Bristol landscape, now converted into bars, offices and flats, to the Afro-Caribbean celebration of St Paul's Festival. The stories that form the heart of this book are slices of that history. They all touch on the south-west in some way, and they are all epic in scope – stories of long journeys undertaken, love lost and found, the barbarity of war and an endless struggle for justice and equality. They are linked by their humanity and by a sense of survival despite often harsh, violent or tragic circumstances. These stories are only glimpses of a huge oral history waiting to be discovered, a fragment of the lives of countless thousands of people living in the south-west whose lives were shaped by empire. Living memory has the ability to bring the past to life – and it can also give us a better understanding of the comings and goings of the British Empire. We hope that this book will act as an encouragement to seek out that history and preserve it.

St Paul's Festival, seen here
e early 1970s.

Hazel Hooper as a young woman.

TWO

DAUGHTER OF INDIA: HAZEL HOOPER

We were only allowed a suitcase, and we were told by the Indian government no money could be taken from India. The English had already taken enough. Who were we to quarrel with that? My husband said, we're living through history.

Ayah, our lovely Ayah. That's what they called them in India. They were nurses and they looked after us, and we just loved them. Mother used to sing a song to us at night, to settle us down. But then she'd go down to dinner, because the gong would go, and she mustn't be late. Ayah would say, 'Go to sleep, my darlings, go to sleep.' And sing her little Indian songs. I remember we loved the smell of coconut in her hair, and the fangaroli flowers tucked up in her little bun. And the jingle of her little glass bracelets. Ayah was always with us. Same routine, put us to bed, wake us up, bath us, take us to the beach. My twin sister, Barbara, and I were born in 1922 and, along with my brother David, lived with my parents in Madras, India. Daddy was a legal adviser to the government, and we lived in a colonial type house with – ooh – fifteen bedrooms? We had ten servants because each wouldn't do each other's job, it was against their caste. The chap who would shake the rugs and beat them on a line, would only do that. The cook would only be the cook. There were probably more than ten in the end. The ten that we paid, maybe they paid one or two to help them.

At Christmas, an elephant would come, quite a small one, decked out with beautiful things, garlands. And on his back, Father Christmas dressed in white, a dhoti and shirt, very black hair, lovely brown skin, and grinning all over his face. And on the side of the elephant would be a sack full of toys. Funny toys some of them, I can tell you, little Indian dolls and sweetmeats, and funny little sticks with funny little whirly things on the top. Mummy would always prepare

Hazel's childhood in British India was full of distractions: 'For entertainment sometimes, the Madras Monkey Man would come, and he'd bring two terrier dogs dressed as horses – little saddles, little reins. And on their backs would be sitting funny little monkeys, dressed like jockeys. And these two monkeys would race round the tennis court, chasing each other. They'd run up poles and do somersaults. We loved it.'

For Hazel and Barbara, their life in British India was one of privilege – in the 1920s motorcars such as this were not common in India or in England.

e house where the twins grew up was typical in its British colonial style. 'Most of us lived in a colonial type
use with – ooh – fifteen bedrooms? Really, each bedroom had its own dressing room. There were
throoms all over the place. And downstairs were enormous rooms, like a ballroom. You could have two
ndred people dancing if you wanted.'

a party, and the servants would come, and our ballroom would be turned into a
room for all the children around. And we'd say 'Father Christmas! Father
Christmas is here!' And when we came back to England some years later, we were
very worried, because he was dressed in red. That wasn't Father Christmas to us,
where was his lovely brown skin and his white dhoti, and where was the elephant?

It was time to leave India when we were six. It was a sad time. I did see Ayah
again years later. But she'd shrunk, or we'd grown. And yet we did recognise
each other. We were sent to Switzerland to school for about a year, and then to
England. This was 1926. When we first got there we were very worried, 'cause
we didn't understand India was so far away. And where was Mummy? I think
they tried to teach us and showed us a map, which meant nothing. And of
course India was painted pink, then. It was terribly strange. Rain, fog, mud. At
school, we worried that the matron was in a very starched get-up. She wouldn't
hold us like Ayah had, and we were put in different dormitories. Well, my twin
sister Barbara and I had never been separated. So we went to the matron and

Dressing up was part of their Indian childhood: 'As a child we only saw the fun side.'

By 1926, the twins had left India by boat to go to boarding school in England – a place that was foreign to them and far away from their parents: 'It was terribly strange. No snow, but rain that came down. It wasn't monsoon, it didn't stop, it just went on as long as it wanted to. And all our English school to learn. But we soon got into the regime of English schoolgirls.'

said, 'Do you think we could have our beds together? We're twins.' And she did put us together, and Barbara and I tried to be good as gold to repay her. Our parents only came back very occasionally to England, because there were no aeroplanes and it took a month or more by boat. Mummy would come every three years. Just for the holidays. And Daddy would come every five years. We weren't allowed to cry, you know, in those days. You hid your feelings. So we suffered together but we didn't tell other people. I really think, looking back and hearing my mother's stories, that she was very broken-hearted. But in those days, wives had to stay with their husbands. They were the hostesses: the servants couldn't manage, goodness knows what would happen to the poor husbands. So Mummy knew she had to divide her time between Daddy and looking after him, and their concerns at Government House. He was the chief adviser to the government and the maharajas all around, and Mummy had to go to all their functions. We understood this, and as we were at boarding school, we knew that Mummy's time was really more important than us. We weren't unhappy, we had each other.

Letters came now and again, which we could read over and over again until they went into sort of ribbons on this thin paper that they used to write on. I've got some of the letters now, in my Bible, and Mummy kept some of our dreadful little writing and drawings. And how we missed Ayah. But what could we do, we had to put up with it. Daddy would have said, 'Come on, you're English, don't cry, stiff upper lip!' That's how we were trained. But I don't think we did bottle it up, because we talked together, and Ayah was alive, and Mummy, Daddy and the servants, and the house. They stayed alive because we talked about them and loved them. Being a twin was a wonderful bonus. When I was at school, they said the British shouldn't be in India, and I though oh dear, what's my father doing? Then I heard about some of the mistakes, especially in the army, that they made against the Indians, which you learn at school. I was rather worried. Because I'd loved the Indians so I couldn't imagine English people doing anything horrid to them. And then of course we learnt about the Black Hole of Calcutta, the Siege of Lucknow and then we were back on the English side.

Then school ended, and we started to embark on the road to India. That was September 1939. When we'd got out into the Atlantic, the boat stopped, all the engines stopped. And then the captain called us to assemble in the ship's drawing room. We thought we knew what he was going to say, because just before we'd got on the ship we'd gone to have tea with Mrs Chamberlain, because she wanted to give some messages to Mummy. Her husband, the Prime Minister, was trying to avert war. But he didn't. When we went to tea she said,

'Don't worry,' she said, 'I don't think there'll be war, I think my husband will stop it, Hitler will listen to him.' But I'm sad to say, as we all know, he didn't. And so we'd guessed what the captain was calling us for. He said, 'I'm so sorry to tell you, that our country is at war with Germany.' Yes, I'm afraid the war had started. Eventually we got to Cochin, where our parents were waiting for us, staring out to sea with binoculars, because we were three weeks late. The telegraph wasn't working. We heard later that the ship had turned around and been sunk on the way back, and everyone on board had been killed.

Our parents decided we should do something for the war. Money was being collected, to raise money for the refugees, and I think to buy half an aeroplane's wing. What could we do? Well, as we'd been trained as dancers and singers,

Even before the Second World War, Britain had begun negotiating the independence of India. But as the Japanese swarmed on the India border in 1942, violence erupted across the continent, when thousands of Indians were killed as they rioted in response to the imprisonment of Gandhi. Hazel and her sister were consumed with raising money for the war, and they put on cabarets all over India. Hazel is second from the right in the left-hand picture, and on the right below.

as well as sportswomen, we began to put on plays. Eventually, Barbara and I started the cabaret that went on at sports clubs. So every Saturday, we'd put on a cabaret. We'd make all our costumes ourselves, designing them and getting tailors to sit on the veranda with little Singer sewing machines – the Singer was famous in India – and they'd sit crossed-legged, whirling it around, all to our patterns. We had to have it ready. That was the order of the day – money, money, money. By then, war was progressing in England at a fast rate, and at last the Japanese were in the war. Daddy said, 'You've got to do what you're told, we're at war now. Stiff upper lip.' I think we were taught very early on to be obedient and not to question our elders, which they can now and quite rightly. We were always taught don't grumble, just get on with it. The English had a saying, stiff upper lip. And it was a joke really. And it went through his life and he taught it us more or less as a joke, just to remind us that even if we didn't like to do something, we did it, because we were asked. 'Remember, stiff upper lip!' And it became half a joke and half a sort of 'Watch it!'

At that time the Madras hospital begged any English woman to come and train as fast as they could. I don't know how they could train us very well, but we could do some of the work. So I started on the wards, three months in this, three months in that, ending up in the operating theatre. And my husband-to-be, Leslie, was one of the wounded. I first met him at Government House, but I was just a schoolgirl, about nineteen years old. I saw this brilliant figure, very handsome figure standing in one of the archways. He came over to me, and for some extraordinary reason he picked me and we danced quite a lot of dances. And like a schoolgirl I fell in love with him, just like that. Like you would a film star or something. First it was he looked completely upright and honest. Very upright. Later I heard from people that they all called him the Nobleman. But he also had this handsomeness, which perhaps as a schoolgirl I saw first!

Well, Leslie came under my jurisdiction in the hospital. And his leg was cut from the top of his leg down to his ankle, down the back of his leg, missing every muscle. And it was my job to pick out the khaki trouser which had got embedded in the wound, which was why the wound was not healing. So he was lying on his front, letting me pick out these threads of khaki trouser. Couldn't see me. I don't think they had many painkillers. No penicillin. Some of the men had to have their legs cut off – quite a different side to life than dancing. Anyway, Leslie turned about and he said 'Good God, it's the sea nymph!' Now he said that because some time before he joined up, he lived with bachelors out by a lake near Madras lagoon. And I was teaching diving then, and they said let's get that girl Hazel to do a diving exhibition, and we'll set a board up.

And I saw there was phosphorescence in the water, and I covered myself with it and ran along the thing to do whatever kind of diving, and I was known as 'the sea nymph'. So when he turned round he saw a poor little creature coming to get khaki cotton out of his wound and he obviously recognized me as the little diver, the sea nymph. And in three months' time we were married. So perhaps that diving did me good, helped me along in life!

He was a lovely man. He was second head of the whole of the railway in India. After our wedding, he got back into civilian life, and I went with him. We lived in a carriage that he commandeered which was really like a little house, which we could hook on to any train and go anywhere. Leslie had to go wherever a train had been derailed, or a bridge had been broken on purpose, or an engine had crashed. He had to be there, and I went with him. I wasn't going to stay away, was I? Stiff upper lip, remember? This lovely carriage. It had a plush drawing room – velvet covers, can you imagine, in the heat? Tassels. Next to it a beautiful bedroom. Then a bathroom, then a kitchen. And then quarters for the cook, the butler and a man who ran about getting things off the station – he'd get you hot milk from the cow. It was a very difficult time, and when we got to the problem, he'd deal with all the people, out in the midday sun. We did that for two years. Up and down India. Got to know India.

At that time Mr Jinnah, who was the Muslim leader, he decided that Pakistan should be kept for the Muslims. And the bottom of India for the Hindus. They didn't like that a bit, 'cause lots of Muslims lived in the south, and they'd never been north. So you can imagine, the turmoil was beginning. And there was the Quit India, which Gandhi had started. And although I respected Gandhi in many ways, the people working for him really became fanatics, and they were beginning to kill the English right, left and centre, whenever they could. The British were going to hand over India, but because of the war, it had to be put off. They couldn't do it during a war. Half the people were joined up in the forces, thousands of Indian troops, wonderful fighters. Gone to France, and later into Germany. So India couldn't really be dealt with then, the government wasn't ready, the Indian government. And if we left in a hurry, we knew there'd be a bloodbath. But Jinnah wanted it in a hurry and Gandhi wanted it in a hurry, and I'm afraid that's what happened. As my father was legal adviser to the Governor, he went to all the Government House dinner parties. We'd listen to Mountbatten, who was a fine soldier but he didn't really know India very well. And he wanted to get partition done quickly. And Mountbatten said, all right let's go ahead, what's to stop us? We've got trains to bring them up and trains to bring them down. And my father said – you can't do it in a hurry. But the

Hazel first met her future husband, Leslie, at a ball at Government House in Madras when she was teenager. 'I saw this brilliant figure, very handsome figure standing in one of the archways. He came over me, and for some extraordinary reason he picked me and we danced quite a lot of dances. Then I went war and I never saw him again until he was on a hospital bed and I was trying to help his wound.' As sl nursed Leslie in an Indian hospital they fell in love, and were married three months later.

fanatics said – this is our chance. We don't want Hindus, kill them wherever you can. And then of course the uprising between the Muslims and the Hindus was beginning. So they started killing each other before they even started their train journeys, out of terror of each other. Fanatics rising up and saying 'Kill the Hindus! Kill the Hindus! They're infidels!' They'd get out of one train that was passing another train on another platform, pull them out and kill them. So the Hindus, with terror, started to do it back, although they weren't quite such a fighting force at that time as the Muslims. But out of sheer fright, they got out their knives, and the bloodbath started.

Leslie and I were in this huge Indian city called Baswada. By now they weren't after the British then, thank goodness, because we'd already said we'd hand over. But I was very fearful for Leslie's life. He was always getting on trains, and he could be very easily killed. And he was very sunburnt by that time, he could have be killed in the muddle. My servants were a mixture, I had Hindus, Christians, Muslims – and they were perfectly good friends, they knew each other from childhood. And now they were a bit frightened, not of each other, but of each other's family. During this time my son was born and actually my husband didn't see him for a month. And when he turned up, was I pleased, not only to see my husband but for him to see our little son. And later, me and the servants and my little boy and his beloved Ayah – another one – had to be housebound. I didn't dare get confused with a Hindu or a Muslim, so I would go on the cart with my white legs sticking out and my high heels – which no Indian would wear – and a very colourful flowered dress, which you could buy on the market. And I would go the market and buy the meat. They soon saw it was an English woman, and they left me alone. Of course we were afraid, but we couldn't show it because we had to give an example. Mummy had lived in the jungle and Daddy had done all sorts of things in this life. Would Daddy show fear? How could I? I've seen a head roll off, a poor Hindu in the wrong place at the wrong time. Tried not to look.

At last we were told that we should leave India. It had been divided, and we were no longer the government. The Indian government took over in 1947. My son then was two years old. So we went to Madras and it was a long journey. I was a blonde, believe it or not, and he was very blonde with hair sticking up all over the place. And we were sitting in a carriage by ourselves. And luckily I said to Ayah – don't go and sit in the servants' carriage. In those days, one's servants travelled in servants' carriages, which weren't so beautiful, I'm sad to say. Didn't have bathrooms and so on. I said, no, come with me. And she did. And it was in between Madras, about four, five hundred miles outside Baswada, and the train was stopped. It wasn't a station, just scrub jungle, no platform, just prickly pear bushes.

I realized that it was Muslims – the Hindus usually waited until you were on the platform. Then they came. I pushed my Ayah – I think I was used to living with fear and acting quickly – I pushed her under the seat, and I hung the baby shawl and some sheets pretending I was drying them. The Indians know how to keep still and quiet, they're brilliant at that. And the door was plucked open with a flourish, and there was this fearful-looking Muslim. And I sat there with my baby. He could have killed me, so what was the point of moving? And I sat there and I faced him. But they had no quarrel with us, but if they'd seen my Ayah they'd have killed her. But luckily she stayed quiet, good little soul she was. Eventually they left. The train started, but with a Hindu who wasn't the driver, who'd been left for dead. He'd got the engine going. Got the water, put the fire on and somehow knew how to pull something. Later we found out that most of the passengers were pulled out and killed. We got to Madras in different trains, a bit shaky and a bit lacking in food. Mummy and Daddy were there to meet us, and then we had to embark on our troop ship.

We were only allowed a suitcase, and we were told by the Indian government no money could be taken from India. The English had already taken enough. Who were we to quarrel with that? My husband said, we're living through history. We stayed on at our own desire to help India, we didn't have to, most of the English people had gone, very few people stayed on. My mother and father had already made provision in England, but we thought we'd be working until Leslie retired. I can see their point, now, looking back. They wanted any wealth that English people had made to stay in India. Why should it go out of India? Why should it? Leslie, who'd lived in India so long, he loved the Indians, and he said, we've got to see both sides of this. He said, we must do what we can for our Indian servants. So we gathered the servants together. They allowed us to take our money out of the bank so long as we didn't take it out of India. We bought little houses along the river in Madras, and gave them to the servants. And every one of them got a monthly pay for the rest of their lives. Only after my husband died did the last one die.

And we didn't know what we were going to do because we had no money, most of what we had was in India. We embarked on this troop ship with one suitcase and a little boy. We had quite a difficult time coming home, terrible weather. We got off at Liverpool and it was snowing. And I had Chinese shoes on with no toes, in Madras you never found boots or shoes. And my little boy, who was only two and a half years old, he said 'Sugar! Sugar!' He'd learnt the

e partition of India into Muslim and Hindu states, which came hand in hand with Indian independence in
47, caused a great deal of bloodshed, although some argue that it averted an even greater civil war. 'During
s time my son was born and actually my husband didn't see him for a month, so he didn't know whether he
s a son or daughter. Leslie went everywhere looking after the railway, and I never knew when I'd see him
ain. . . . Eventually we were told that we must leave India, and leave the Indian railway to run itself.'
s photograph was taken in December 1946, when their son was three months old.

word sugar and thought it was coming down, and was trying to catch sugar in his hand! We got to our friends, a big house, and then we had to think what we were going to do. We had a little money in the bank, it really wasn't much, about a thousand pounds. So we rented a farm. What got into us to rent a farm, we'd never touched soil in our lives! We didn't know anything about animals except the cows that came to be milked in our compound, or monkeys. But Leslie had read about it, on the boat. He said, you could learn to cook – agggh! Terrifying thought! I didn't know how to cook anything, I didn't know how to boil an egg!

We had to buy English clothes, with coupons and very little money. Leslie laughed and he said, 'I say, it's really rather like going from riches to rags.' We imagined ourselves with all our beautiful ball dresses and his dinner suits, suddenly ending up on the farm wearing any old clothes. We rented this farm in Sussex. About eighty-four acres, and it already had animals on it. I'd never made a bed in my life, I'd never ironed. But it was the cooking. First I had to go and find the food in a shop. 'Course I'd bargain – what! I soon learnt that wasn't on. So I learnt the English way and I learnt the English money. Every day was an adventure. Another farmer funnily enough had been in Kenya, so he didn't know English farming either. And his wife did know a little bit about cooking. And she used to bring Mrs Beeton's book over, which I'd study all night like a novel. I must make a cake! Eventually I got it right, and we'd all sit round this cake and say it was marvellous, whether it was or not.

In India, we'd often talked about being shipwrecked, what we would do. We'd say, we'd look for shelter, and hope to find this. We just used to talk about it. So when we got to England, we'd say, let's pretend we're shipwrecked. We haven't got much money, we've got to make do. We've got to make a door out of planks of wood we'd found. We'd bought some nails cheap, they might have been a bit rusty. We really did everything on the cheap. Leslie even made a pigsty later; he learnt to put bricks one on top of the other. At first it didn't work, but gradually we got it right or bought a book about it. So it was rather like our desert island stories. A desert island, without much money, without proper tools. But what we found, we made use of. He was that sort of man who made fun out of everything, and had the stiff upper lip. And I hope I copied him. And we ran a market garden, which I absolutely loved, because I was very supple and very strong, and I never seemed to get tired. There were all the new things to pick, tiny lettuces, strawberries. We had to take it to Covent Garden. Leslie bought a dreadful old truck that sort of did hiccups all the way, which he taught me to drive. Off we'd go from Sussex to London, which took us hours,

I can say, getting petrol on the way. We'd start before midnight and we'd get there at about half past five in the morning, to get our strawberries or blackcurrants to market on time. I'd always go with him, with my little boy, and then my new baby was born, so he had to come too. So a little two-year-old and new baby went trucking up and down to Covent Garden at five in the morning. We did that for four years.

Leslie got a good job in the end. Then he died at the age of sixty-three, and he was still looking terribly well and strong and tall. I moved to Bristol to be near my son and his family. I bought this little house in Redland, near the shops, and near a bus, and near the schools so that I could look after the grandchildren. I taught them songs and taught them to tap dance. We've had such fun, it's made my life. But still, I suppose because I lived so long in India, as did my family, a lot of India is in me. The music, the people, they're with me all the time. And of course I knew I had to be English, I tried to be English, and sometimes I failed. I sometimes feel I'm in the wrong country, yet of course I know I'm not. My family are very, very English, and I do uphold England. At the time I didn't think of us ruling India, I thought of us more as colleagues.

Hazel Hooper in India
in the late 1940s.

Hazel Hooper died in June 2003, giving this interview a few months before she died.

Precious McKenzie today.

THREE

ESCAPING APARTHEID: PRECIOUS MCKENZIE

When she discovered that I'd just missed that lift and had a next lift to come, the Queen said, 'We'll leave when he's finished.' That was the biggest moment in my life.

I was born in Durban in 1936; however, later we moved to Pietermaritzberg. I was the sickliest child of all my mother's children. I caught double pneumonia, but I survived. Eventually, when I had to be baptized, my mother said, 'Seeing as you were the sickliest child of my four children, I will name you my Precious son.' That's how I got my name. My sister Gloria and I we were practically the same size in growth so we did look like twins – everybody thought we were twins. When my father, who was a hunter, was eaten by a crocodile in the Limpopo River, I think from then onwards things happened to my mother. She couldn't bring up the four children, couldn't cope. But fortunately my two brothers were old enough to be sent to a convent – St Theresa's in Durban. My sister and myself, the Welfare Society took over.

We were given to foster parents. Now in those days I think foster parents weren't given children because they loved kids. They were given the children as a business agreement. The person that we were given to was in Natal. She was Alice. Alice had a beautiful house, and in the yard at the back she had a beautiful farm situation with fruit trees – quince, and I can't recall all the others. So when the Welfare Society put us to this lady to look after us, it did look heaven when she took us. And I can recall the Welfare Society gave us all this beautiful clothing. I had a suit, a soldier's suit, with a cane and a cap. When my sister talks about that, she says that I loved the suit so, that if I had my way I would sleep in it.

We had chores. We had to get water from a mile away – 'cause there was no taps in those days. We used to get the water from a sort of pump. We'd pump the water out into a four-gallon bucket. All the other African women and bigger children would come there to collect this water. But being so tiny, we couldn't actually put the water on our heads. So these people would help us – put it on a fence, and then on a pole and then on our heads. And then we would have to walk a mile with this water. At that age, there was no way we could handle this sort of thing. The drum fell from our head, and as it fell, the seam in the side of it has cracked. When it cracks you lose most of the water. Punishment would arrive now. Our foster mother Alice said that we have to go and get these sticks. We had to pick about seven quince sticks, now it could've been five, six, whatever, we couldn't count. But we brought these sticks. Then she undresses us completely naked, and we had an old bed there. She tie us up on this bed on our stomachs, and then of course, thrashed me with this stick on the back. If that stick breaks, she gets another one, until those sticks were completely broken. Now I will be bleeding everywhere, on my back, everywhere. So my sister's turn comes along. After that punishment, she let us sit at the back of the kitchen door. We had to sit there the whole night. Now, it was very scary for children to sit there, so we're sitting there crying all the time. The scary part is when you hear the owls, the sound of the owls. We think it's ghosts, because we're told about ghosts. I tell you, it was really scary.

Alice thought there must be something wrong with us, because we couldn't carry the water. So she must go to a witch doctor and the devil must get out of us. She took us one day. The witch doctor looked like a normal fella, dressed normally. And he was a bit educated too, so they believed him more. Those days, they made money out of the fools. So, the doctor takes a razor blade, and make small cuts in all of our joints, I still got the marks here. See, he nips so blood will come out. And they have this black medicine and they shove it in every joint, even on top of the head, the feet, every joint. We were terrified. They're praying over you to get all the devils out of you. That's the sort of belief they had. We didn't really believe it. While that was happening my sister and I were screaming to ourself, where's our mother? We were hoping that she would come and get us. We didn't know then that my mother got married. She married Mr Nicholson, and he was European. An ex-soldier. An ex-pilot in the last world war. And he had all his medals for bravery and all this sort of thing.

Gloria and myself used to go to Sunday School. When these people discover all these sores we had on our bodies, and on our legs as well, they reported that to the Welfare Society. So the Welfare Society decided that they would find out

oys help out one of the monks at Van Rhynsdorp Catholic Mission, where Precious and his sister were sent the 1950s. Precious is the boy with the guitar on the far left.

when this lady would be going to the city and that's the day they will come get us. That's the only way they could get us, was to steal us – that's how cruel she was. The nicest part about it is that when they came and picked me up from the school my sister was in the car, and it was such a glory thing to happen to us to sit in a beautiful motorcar and be driven away. It was something I couldn't describe. They drove us straight to the Welfare doctor. When he came to my clothing, they couldn't take the shirt and the vest off because all the blood and so on it stuck to the clothing. The doctor had to use water to get the skin from the vest and the shirt.

After that, the Welfare Society said it was the best thing for our education if we were sent away to the Catholic Mission. It was a dramatic departure, and it was a long journey – a week on the train. Unfortunately we were separated from our mother, that was a sad situation there, but once kids are on a train it was heaven. And you could never see two happier children in a train going away, it was quite a journey. We end up at Van Rhynsdorp Catholic Mission, and we were looked after by nuns and by monks and priests. We had a good time there.

Precious (left) with his mother Christina and his brother Leslie, who was a boxer. By the late 1950s, when thi was taken, African states such as Kenya and Ghana were beginning to free themselves from the chains c empire. But while they were gaining independence, South Africa's new leader, Dr Verwoerd, was tightenin the grip of apartheid, officially begun in 1948, by making it even more segregationist.

But we had no shoes. The welfare used to send to convents old clothes, we used to have all these clothes from England, from everywhere. My feet used to be frozen, so I wanted a pair of shoes. As we went among the clothing there, you could pick what you want, so I saw a pair of ladies shoes, and there's high heels. I broke all these high heels, I broke them off completely. And I fit my feet into these shoes – and that was the best shoes I've ever owned! And guess what happened to the shoe eventually? Because my feet were smaller than the shoes themselves, the toes started to curl up. And it was really funny walking round in these shoes. Really funny!

Food was very little. We used to get up every morning, the nuns wake us up at half past five. We'd wash our faces and then go to mass. Have our breakfast and it's porridge. The porridge was mealie-meal. I don't know if you know what that is. It is corn meal, ground up. Of course, the food wasn't sufficient. We were always hungry. And when you used to go in the desert walking around, there's tortoise. The older guys used to catch these tortoise and cruelly, to me it was cruel even then, they put the tortoise on the fire and of course eventually the tortoise want to get out. But when he comes out he finds there's fire, so he goes back in. And that's how they kill the tortoise. I think it's a very bad death. However, then they used to break the tortoise up and feed us tortoise meat. The boys in our dormitory used to escape at night to go and raid bins of the food that they were throwing there. That's how bad things were for us. Today I couldn't comprehend that. My sister and I were very slow in our growth now. We were not having sufficient nourishment. If you look at today's children they grow big fast, very quickly. My grandson is six foot and weighs a hundred and fifty kilos. But my sister and I, we stunted our growth because we lacked vitamins. Our growth was really affected that way and that's why we were the smallest among all the other children. They used to call you Shorty. Now that word was very insulting as a child. I must say, I had a fight. Constant fight. Bigger boys wanted to bully me. But I'm afraid they didn't succeed because, for my age, I was strong. I wouldn't let anyone get on top of me. And my sister was always next to me, we worked as a team.

My sister and I used to be very hungry, we used to get hungry the two of us. We used to go on the streets, do some acrobats, with some Indian people. To get some food, you see. And we used to sing this song:

Poor little Johnny
His mother is dead
His father is a loafer
He couldn't buy his bread.
He sits by the window
And play his banjo
And thinks about his mother
Far, far away.

Every time we run into problems, and we're sitting there on our own, my sister and I, we're thinking about our mother, nobody else. We look at a sky, the cloud's moving, we picture our mother's there. We picture our mother's gonna come. We write a letter to her, we don't get a reply. And eventually we get a reply. Man, it boosts us, immediately! We'll take this letter and read it over and over and over. And then we'll write letters again, again no reply. 'Cause we had to send the letters to the Welfare, to find our where she is.

I was lucky. One of the Dutch priests had a horizontal bar built, and some ropes. I was starting doing all these acrobatics. The priest used to show us some movies, and then we used to see the circus. And that's where it came to my mind. Hey, I can do that! I can succeed in that. I want to be one of those acrobatic guys. When I eventually left the convent in 1954, and got to my hometown of Pietermaritzberg, I knew I wanted to do acrobatics. So I went to the circus and got there, and saw these fellas doing all the tumbling work at the back. Do you know what I did? I went up to them and started doing tumbling work. Now because I'm coloured, in South Africa then you were nothing, you had no opportunities whatsoever. So when I did all the tumbling so good, they just ignored me. Eventually they said, get away.

So I found a gym. I went up there, but guess what, it wasn't a gym for gymnastics, it was a weightlifting gym. I did gymnastics. I used to get on the bar, seven foot high, and do a back somersault there, I used to always wait until there's nobody there. That's the worst thing you can ever do! 'Cause anything could happen to me there – break my neck, no ambulance, nobody's there. I was getting happy! I persevered, and a man saw me doing this every day and he said why don't you join the weightlifters here, that'll be very good for your gymnastics. I fell for it! So I became a weightlifter by accident, total accident. Then I did some bodybuilding and won my first trophy as Mr West End. From there onwards I was lifting weights and nothing stopped me.

I won the Natal championships and from there the South African championships. I became the best weightlifter in the whole country. But in South Africa the apartheid law was so strong, so powerful and so regimentally done it worked dramatically. Because not only were you segregated by European and coloured. It was worse than that. The Indian, coloured, African couldn't mix either. We were segregated as well. The coloured was higher than the Indian, and the Indian was higher than the Bantu, which is African. So you can see we can now discriminate among ourselves. Can you see how the system works? But the environment in which we grew up was to teach us that's the way we should live. And I didn't want to live that way.

Now with the apartheid law, we blacks weren't allowed to represent the country in sport. There were separate organisations. Black South Africans and White South Africans. Meanwhile they're telling the outside world that we blacks weren't good enough, that's the reason that we never get selected. But as a South African champion my total was better than my white opponent. When the Olympic games came along in 1958, my white opponent was selected to go to the Commonwealth games. He won a gold medal for South Africa in Cardiff

cious trained hard and by 1959 he was setting weightlifting records at the South African championships.
 apartheid meant that he could not compete for his country or join certain important sports bodies
ause he was black. 'I could see there's discrimination and this is not right, without being taught. I
ember at that time I knew nothing about politics, but you can see that I'm growing up with the mentality
aying that we're equal. I thought, I'm not inferior.' South African sports were boycotted around the world,
 by 1961 South Africa had been kicked out of the Commonwealth. It was excluded from the Tokyo
mpics in 1964, but its adherence to apartheid showed no signs of weakening.

in 1958. I couldn't comprehend that, how could they get away with that? And that's why the Olympic movement in South Africa was trying to fight it, that's when we formed the South African Multiracial Committee and things went on. The press was starting to bark loud and clear that here was a black South African who's the best in the country, and he's international standard. Why is he left out? Those were the questions that couldn't be answered. But I said to myself, if they can boast about me, how good I am, and I cannot go and prove myself, it's like a finished story. So get out there and show the world. I was working for Barker's Shoes. Mr Taylor, who was the managing director of the company, used to like me. So I thought to myself, take advantage of this. My little brain says to me, approach him one day and ask him because we have a sister company in Northampton, England called Crockett and Jones, it belongs to Barker's Shoes. I thought to myself, why don't you go to him and see if you can get a work permit? He got me the permit. Now I could apply for my passport.

But they wouldn't give me a passport. I made the application, but they called me to the security branch office for interrogation. 'Why do you want to go to England?' They had a lamp right in front of you; you sit there with these two guys. They look you in the eye, interviewing you. They wanted to see if I was involved in politics or anything like that. Mandela was now in jail, you see. No, they could see I was clean. But during the interrogation they were trying to put me off by saying, 'You know what, you know there's apartheid in England – they're worse than us!' He was trying to brainwash me. 'At least here, we will tell you in your face that you're black, and put you in your place, but not in England.'

My passport didn't arrive on the day that I was sailing. I was extremely worried. All my friends, the Weightlifters' Association, came to see me off, at the docks. And I had no passport. So that morning, the very first thing I done, I went to the city to go and find out where my passport was. They said to me, your passport has been sent. Go home, they said, you'll find it in your letterbox. That was the kind of situation they put you in. They thought you would go home and cancel your trip. But I still had the feeling that I would get it, and when I got home I found it! Straight way, I ran and got on that ship.

When I got to Britain, Northampton was all right, that wasn't too bad. I remember sitting in the buses and sitting next to a white person, this was all new to me. At the cinema, I didn't know where to sit – no black and white areas. And I sat down and I felt so guilty. And someone said to me, you know what, you're not in South Africa now. You're in England! Forget about that. I sat back and relaxed. I thought to myself – this is a new world.

By now I was married to Elizabeth, my wife. We had children, two by then. She was following three months later. But by the time I got the passport for my wife to come here, I'd already written to my wife. I said, look, I want to come back home to South Africa. I can't find accommodation for us. The obstacles were: you've got children, number one, you wouldn't get a flat. And number two: you were black, you wouldn't get a flat. I said, darling, I have to come back, this is not working out. She replied to me – that's why I've got such great respect for my wife, she had guts – she stuck to what we said, that through thick and thin we would not come back to South Africa. That was the only time that I nearly break down. My wife replied, 'You said through thick and thin the two of us will stick together. I am coming.' That's the whole reason I'm sitting here talking to you today, because of my wife.

By the mid-1960s Nelson Mandela and his fellow ANC leaders were in prison, and it was clear to Precious, like many other black sportsmen and women in South Africa, that the only way to succeed was to leave the country. He moved with his family first to Northampton, then to Bristol, where he began training at the famous Empire Gym. 'That was the beginning of beginnings. Bristol took me with open arms immediately.'

Here we are struggling just to get a flat, get a room. And you just had a lump in your throat to think you went through all this in your life and you are still having the battles. I approached these Pakistani fellows, and they helped us. We had this one room with a pianola in it. We had our Christmas dinner on our lap, my wife and I. Two children, on the floor, eating the Christmas dinner. Would you believe it, that was the happiest time in our life, sitting on a bed there. The evening of Boxing Day, I opened the door to put the milk bottles out . . . first time in our life we ever saw snow! Tremendous excitement went on. I ran inside, went to the wife, woke the children up, by golly, we picked up the snow, ate the snow.

Eventually I went from Northampton to Bristol. The government had a redeployment scheme, and I was prepared to move. That was the beginning of beginnings. Bristol took me with open arms immediately. The *Evening Post* made a fuss about my name. The place that I trained, that I was introduced to, was the Empire Gym, in St Paul's. And by golly it's a lovely place, up to this very day. I joined there, Den Welch was running the gym. And that gym was

In the early days, when Precious was working as a leather cutter in Bristol, he used to run to the gym every day – but eventually bought himself a bicycle.

When the Empire Gym was closed, Precious would train at home; here he is with his son Quinton.

Precious was very popular in Bristol, and had a great deal of support from local newspapers, as this still fr[...] the *Bristol Evening Post* shows.

cious met Mohammed Ali in 1974.

never touched even during the riots, and you've never seen such a beautiful mixture. My training regime was so harsh. My regime was that I never stopped training. During the Easter-time the gym was closed. I used to bring my weights to my house, I'd bench-press and squat the weights in my kitchen! My neighbours used to hear the weights hitting the floor and they used to hit the wall. In other words, stop those weights, you're gonna break down the whole place! I had to stop using the weights – so I used to pick up my wife, and sometimes the children, and put them on my shoulder and practise lifting them, instead of the weights!

When I won my first gold medal for England in Jamaica [at the Commonwealth games], they played this national anthem. I sang it. But believe you me, the tears rolled out of my eyes. It wasn't the joy only, it was the sadness combining with the joy, telling me that here is a country, a white country, that took me with open arms. Not because of my colour, but because of what I can do, what I can do for the country. And yet, my own birth country wouldn't accept me because I had the wrong colour according to them. And that hit me so hard, that those tears were for joy and sadness. That very first medal.

The most particular moment that hit me more hard than anywhere else was making the fourth consecutive gold medal, and the Queen being there to watch me winning and making history. But believe you me, at this particular moment I was getting cramp. I went for that lift. And I missed it. My winning lift. Now the Queen always goes to every event for a certain time, her schedule is completely pinned to time. But when she discovered that I'd just missed that lift and had a next lift to come, the Queen said, 'We'll leave when he's finished.'

That was the biggest moment in my life. When I failed that one, something said to me, Precious, there is no such thing now as pain. There's nothing on the bar. Go and grab it, get it up there. The pressure was dramatic now, because there's the Queen waiting there, for me to do this lift. And everyone watching, will this man do it or not? Because he just failed. But by golly, when I went there, picked it up, got it up to here [chest height], and when I got out I could feel the cramp wanting to come. I drove that weight. When I held it up there and the ref said put it down – well, I did that and then jumped in the air. And I had to stop straight away because I was told not to move since the Queen was leaving! Then I jumped up and made this sign [holds four fingers up]. The fourth gold medal, no one had ever done it.

...us won four consecutive gold medals at the Commonwealth games, a record at the time. Here he is in ... at the 1972 Olympic games in Munich, weightlifting in the bantamweight category. (*Popperfoto.com*)

Son Quinton holds up the envelope from Buckingham Palace announcing Precious's MBE in 1974.

Precious McKenzie was noted for his strong stand against apartheid in South Africa and its exclusion of black athletes in its national teams. After living in Bristol for many years, he later moved to New Zealand, where he still lives. However, he still considers Bristol his English home and visits often, still training at the Empire Gym. He is sixty-seven.

Precious McKenzie's
Sporting Achievements

Nine times British Weightlifting Champion
Ten times British Powerlifting Champion
Five times World Powerlifting Champion

Four consecutive gold medals
at the Commonwealth games

Represented Britain at the Olympic games:
Mexico (1968)
Munich (1972)
Montreal (1976)

Current World Masters
Powerlifting Champion (2003)

Presented with an MBE
by the Queen in 1974

Rosalind Balcon today.

FOUR

OUT OF AFRICA: ROSALIND BALCON

And you see this awful orange envelope. You just know that something dreadful has happened. And I opened it and I don't honestly remember going from the box to the car. But I do remember the dog – I had a border collie. He started licking me and making a great fuss.

We weren't very impressed when my parents came back and told us that we were all going out to live in East Africa. I have a twin sister, and we were both thinking, well they must be mad, what on earth do they want to go out to this horrible place for? This was 1935, and I was nearly thirteen. A girl at school told me that her father had been in Uganda, and she had been there as well, and she said, 'They have spiders as big as dinner plates, how're you going to cope with that?' But my father was in the First World War, and he felt he could see another war coming. He didn't want his family to be involved in it because he realized that bombing would be a big part of it. We had a very interesting journey out, we just loved it. Especially getting into Port Said, 'cause in those day the bumboats came all round, selling wares, a lot of leatherwork and that sort of thing. And the gulli-gulli men came aboard – the gulli-gulli men had little chicks, and they would suddenly bring out one from the left ear, and you'd look, and before long they'd got one from the right ear, and one from your pocket. It was absolutely amazing. It was wonderful.

My father had bought the Blue Post Hotel at Thika. That had rather primitive conditions. We had no running water – well we had running water but there were no proper loos or anything like that, it was all a bucket system. We had electricity, but I remember that most of the sitting room of the main building was made of earth, I suppose – wattle, daub. Most of the people who came through were commercial travellers perhaps, particularly from the

Rosalind and her sister, pictured here with their mother in England, were thirteen when their parents decid
to emigrate. 'First of all they tried the Bahamas, and they decided that wasn't for them, and then they hea
a talk about Kenya. They went out, on a sort of recce, and spent about four months out there, and qu
decided that that was where they were going to settle.'

Rosalind's father bought the Blue Post Hotel at Thika, Kenya. 'We had no running water – well we
running water but there were no proper loos or anything like that, it was all a bucket system. We
electricity, but I remember that most of the sitting room of the main building was made of earth, I suppc
wattle, daub.' The hotel still survives today.

commercial companies, petrol companies. Tobacco people, that sort of thing. The Blue Post is – and still has – two very large rivers which converge at a point, so it's a rather triangular piece of ground. One of them is the Chania Falls, a very beautiful falls. The hotel was placed so that one could see this, and it was marvellous, with very tall trees. My mother put orchids in the trees – beautiful. There were hippos in the river, and snakes. We've seen leopards there, monkeys. It was really a wonderful place.

We were sent to boarding school at a place called Limuru, which was higher up, about seven and a half thousand feet. We enjoyed our time there enormously. From my desk, and I always tried to get the same desk, at the back (so no one could see that I wasn't working), you see right across to Kilimanjaro. And Kilimanjaro in the sunset is really something. Because then it had a lot of snow on it and it turned pink. It was at a time when things were in a bad way in

ing their first years in Kenya Rosalind and her twin sister adapted very quickly to African life. 'Hippo were in river and would come up at night. They'd empty the dustbins, and things like that. And the staff – who e in a compound really – they complained bitterly, they were frightened of these things. With good reason!'

Kenya, they'd had locusts several years running. And the locusts are terrible. They came when we were at the school, and you literally could see this cloud coming up the valley, and then before they arrived you got these scouts, these great big huge grasshopper things. But when they really arrived, they were just everywhere. And we had a ridge near the school where we had some cedar trees growing. They landed on those, and by morning most of the trees had been stripped to branches, literally from the weight of the locusts. But that had a terrible effect on the farmers because everything was absolutely ruined. They knocked down the branches as well as eating everything that was on it. Everything was just simply stripped. And then they moved on. The Africans used to come out with drums and tins and things and try and chase them off but of course it really made no difference. They used to roast them and eat them.

Plagues of locust were common in Kenya in the 1930s: 'I remember, playing tennis. You just hit locust instead of the ball, it was really rather fun! But that had a terrible effect on the farmers because everything was absolutely ruined.'

The famous Chania Falls in Kenya, near the hotel where Rosalind grew up.

My father was a very, very straight Victorian teetotaller. Quite amazing for somebody who ran a successful hotel! He wouldn't even have sherry trifle, because it had sherry in it! So you had to just say it was a trifle and forget about the sherry part. He was also rather strict about his daughters. Not without justification, I have to admit. My mother's heart gave up and she was told that she couldn't live at Thika because it was too high – she must go and live at the coast. So down she went. My twin and I took turns looking after mother. By this time we had just left school, at sixteen we left school. So I suppose I was probably seventeen, eighteen by this time. And that was when I first met John, because he came into the hotel. We spoke, and after that things got from bad to worse, and we fell in love. I fell in love with his looks, and I fell in love with his personality. He was very confident, and that was something I lacked. I always imagined, and believed, that anyone could do what I could do very much better.

Much to her father's chagrin, Rosalind met her husband John at the Blue Post Hotel at Thika when he was young soldier, and although she was forbidden to see him at first, they later married in 1941.

Rosalind's husband John, on their honeymoon.

It's something that's just dogged me all my life. John was very knowledgeable, he'd been to Cambridge, he'd talk about things that I'd only heard about. But my father was very, very against anything like that, you had to keep these chaps very much at a distance. However, we had a dance one night. We used to have it every Saturday night, roll back the carpet in the dining room, put on the gramophone with 78s, and that was the way we did it. It was great fun. And my father found us out in the garden. He said, 'If the dance floor isn't good enough, you can go to bed!' I said the dance floor's quite good enough thank you. He said, 'You can go to bed!' So off I had to go. He told John that he must never see me again, that he didn't want to see him at the hotel again, and that if he didn't go, he'd get out his rifle and chase him off. John was in a state, and I said, forget about it, leave it, and I raced for my bedroom. And the next thing I knew John was at the bedroom window saying, this can't happen, this can't happen, I have to see you again. And of course somehow I did see him again. But we thought John was going to Burma, which he should have done, he was supposed to go on the drafts that went off but for some reason was hauled off and sent to another battalion. And the battalion happened to be in Mombasa – he couldn't believe his luck. We got together then, and we were married.

Eventually he was sent to Burma. Soon after, I was told that he was missing, been killed. I was living in Mombasa then, and my daughter Vicky had been born in 1942, in Nairobi. So I was at home looking after her in my mother's house, although my parents were actually away at the time. You go to the post office and you look for letters, we always had a box where nothing was delivered. And you see this awful orange envelope. You just know that something dreadful has happened. And I opened it and I don't honestly remember going from the box to the car. But I do remember the dog – I had a border collie – and he started licking me, and making a great fuss. I suppose I was making noises, I don't know. And I remember someone coming up and saying, 'What's the matter?' and I gave her the telegram, and she said, 'You mustn't give up hope. It'll go right.' But we knew what the Japanese would do if they got hold of anybody.

Eventually I received a letter from him. It was just unbelievable. My friend said, 'Now just hold it a minute. That letter could have been sent before he died.' But it wasn't, and I confirmed it with his echelon, and he really was alive. But he'd had a bad time. They knew some Japs were in the area and they went out to scout to see what was going on. And the Japs spotted them and he got separated from his patrol, with just his African sergeant. They eventually found what they thought was headquarters, just sort of casually went in, only to discover that in fact they were in a Japanese camp. They hastily beat their

November. '42.

To Rosalind — becau[se] I adore you.

John Balcon in November 1942. The photograph is inscribed 'To Rosalind, because I adore you.'

This was taken in Port Tudor in August 1943, around the time of Vicky's first birthday.

retreat but they'd been spotted, and they had to hide in the bamboo. They were very thirsty and they had to try and get water from pieces of bamboo where it had sort of settled. He told me that if it hadn't been for this African chap he would never have got out. But they did survive and they managed to get back to where their division was, and they walked back into camp, but by that time he'd been reported missing and I'd got my letter. It was utterly devastating. You're there, there's blue sky, it's wonderful, you're feeling absolutely on top of the world, you go to the post office thinking, well, I know there's going to be a letter there today, and you get this awful news.

But! We got over that, and John came back from Burma. Eventually, the war ended, and we went where the army sent us. By 1948 we were in a place called Belet Uen in what had been Italian Somaliland. We had our very first house there, and we were extremely happy. We found that we could buy all sorts of things there, such as occasionally bread, and that sort of thing. Of course you still had to go down and get things from Mogadishu, but we could manage all right. Now at that time the region was being handed back to the Ethiopians.

It had been annexed by the Italians and was now going to be handed back. One day, John said he must go up to a place called Dolo. He went up as part of an extra patrol, to help out, and while he was there I actually went to see him. I shouldn't have done, but I did. I'd asked for permission to go there and was told it wasn't possible. So when this other officer said, 'Would you like to go? I'm going up for one day', really and truly I should have said no, but I suppose again the old determination to do the wrong thing took over, and I went. I know that the captain, he said, 'You shouldn't be here, there's no accommodation for ladies. And the others haven't got their spouses here so we don't really need you!' He was absolutely right. But we had a lovely long walk along the river, and watched crocodiles on a big island in the river. They're quite fascinating things to watch. We had a room, and we sat in there after we'd had our meal, and then the next morning we were off pretty early. I remember turning back and he wasn't even looking, he was getting on with his work.

Soon after that I woke up one night and thought that I could hear the trucks coming back. He'd said to me, don't worry, it won't be long before we're back, they're sending people back all the time now. And I thought they were coming back. The next morning I know I was very busy sewing because I was making a shirt for him. A girl who I didn't know – I knew she was the policeman's wife, but I hadn't got to know her at all. She came up the steps looking absolutely white and she was sobbing. And well, I sat her down and gave her a brandy, I thought I'd better recover this poor woman, I didn't know what had happened. And she then blurted out, 'Your husband's been killed, he's dead.' Of course, I didn't believe her, partly because she was half-hysterical, and partly because I thought the Company Commander, who I knew well, would come and tell me. But I think, it isn't an easy thing to do, and he thought it would be easier if I heard it from another woman.

I couldn't believe it, I couldn't believe that he was really dead. I thought, this isn't true, can't be. He's too alive. You're young, you're in love, you just don't want to believe it. So I went to see the Company Commander. He said he was afraid it was true, they were bringing John down to be buried. He'd been caught in an ambush. And then I saw a burial party coming back. I remembered that just before John had left, he'd said that he wouldn't like to be buried in Somalia. I suppose he didn't really mean it, he never thought he'd be buried there. So I said to the CC, 'He's not going to be buried here – it's not to be here.' He said, all right, he'd make arrangements that it'd be in Mogadishu. I insisted on seeing the body. I remember walking down from the house with the doctor, and I know the tears were falling down my face, because I was beginning to take it on board by then I suppose and I remember the doctor saying to me, 'Pull yourself together Rosalind, what would John think if he saw you like this?' And I did. And I remember going into this room and there was a nun there, and I resented that, I wanted to be alone, wanted to be quite private. He had been shot through the neck, and there was blood on his nostrils and on his lips. It wasn't a happy sight. It's a sight you never forget, and I should not have seen it. It was my fault, I insisted, they did their best to persuade me not to go and see him but I insisted upon it. And I just wanted to be with that body, but you know immediately you see a body, that that person is gone. They're dead. They have gone.

The doctor then said, you shall be leaving for Mogadishu, where John will be buried, in half an hour. So I packed a suitcase, and gathered the children, and off we went. All through the night, which was horrible. I was sent up to the cemetery. And we had the burial next morning. I think that hearing the Last Post has always meant more to me than to a lot of people. Because anyone who's buried their husband, and hears that Last Post, it always brings it back, it's bound to. Ten weeks later, I went back to the cemetery to say one last farewell and went down to South Africa to meet my parents, who had bought this small hotel in George, in South Africa. When we arrived, I think it struck me then that life would never be the same again and that part of it was gone. Gone forever. But having said that, I didn't get over it for three, maybe four years. I told the children their father had gone to heaven. Now, for Guy, literally, two years and one week, he didn't understand at all, it meant nothing to him. Vicky had become extremely attached to her father and it meant a great deal to her, but I decided that I would never let them see me cry because I knew that would upset them. And she would say, 'Is Daddy all right in heaven?' And I would say yes, he's perfectly all right. He's waiting for us to get there one day – it'll be a long time, sort of thing. I knew it was a good thing to have a jolly good cry, but I always did it in the bath, so that they didn't know anything about it. It was a terrible, terrible loneliness. It's something you just can't conceive until you are widowed.

I don't think the business of starting another life hit me until I got to South Africa. I was lucky to have my parents, who could offer me a roof over my head. But I found that living with father was not very easy. Not only was I not allowed to have a drink, of course, but he was very strict about other things too. I was there for two or three years, but couldn't settle and went back to Kenya, best thing I ever did. I was lucky enough to join the police, and that meant I was made a radio operator with the Kenyan Police. We lived very simply then, with next to nothing, but we had the tiniest little house, it was twenty foot by

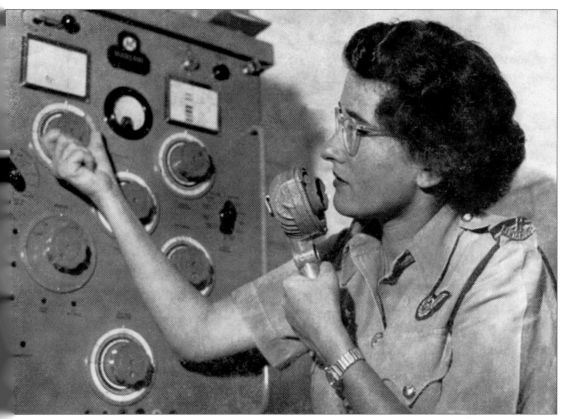

osalind eventually returned to Kenya after her husband's death in 1948, and for many years she worked as a dio operator in Nakuru. It was there that she met John's cousin Mike, whom she later married: 'I think the ct that he was part of John's family undoubtedly was a great attraction, I knew I was on safe ground. But I st knew that this would be all right. I don't know why, I can't really say. It has proved to be all right, and at's all that matters at the end of the day.'

thirty, and that included a bathroom and kitchen, a small bedroom and a living room. But we lived happily.

One day I had a letter from my mother-in-law to say that cousin Mike – who was John's cousin – was in Kenya. This is his number, get in touch with him. So I sent him a letter saying, come and have some tea. That was September 1958. Well, I didn't hear anything. Then suddenly just before Christmas I get a letter saying, I'm coming over. So fix me up a room in the mess. Because he knew where I was. So I did. And I went and met him in Nairobi and picked him up and brought him back. We just treated each other as very much cousins, but Christmas came, and he was only there about ten days. I was working in a bank by then, my daughter was on holiday from school and Guy was in England at school. And well, we just had a very good time over Christmas, and we fell in love.

Mike, who was very impetuous, was quite determined that we should get married straight away. I said we couldn't possibly do it because the children were at school, holidays were coming up, Easter and so on. Perhaps after Easter we'd talk about it. The next thing I knew I had thirty-six red roses sent to me, which I'd never had sent to me before, which quite impressed me, and I also had letters saying he couldn't live without me and all this sort of thing. We'd only known each other really for about ten days. And then suddenly the bank manager came and said there was a phone call: 'Very squeaky line and it's for you. Better take it in my office.' Wasn't often we were invited into the office of, you know, high-ups! And it was a chap who said he'd had a signal from Aden, and that Mike was coming over, and I was to book him a hotel, the following week for two nights. And I thought, 'After all that he's coming over for a dirty weekend! Well, he can't do that!' So I signalled back, 'Is this marriage or not?' And he came back with the answer, 'Yes, it is!' I'd had several proposals of marriage, which I'd turned down. But I just knew that this would be all right. I don't know why, I can't really say.

Rosalind and Mike in 1995 at home in Somerset.

Rosalind and Mike on their fortieth wedding anniversary.

So he came over on the Thursday, and we were married that same day by the VC in Nairobi. Then he said, 'I think you'd better come back with me to Aden.' The bank gave me permission to leave immediately – I think they must have been frightened of me! I packed up the house, found somewhere for the horses, and the cat and the dog, everything, left the house within a week and went to Aden. It was great. We had a year in Aden, back to England for a short visit, and then off to Hong Kong with the battalion. Even though they were cousins, he wasn't a bit like John and when I mentioned this to my mother she said, 'Well, I'm glad to hear it. I wouldn't like to think that you'd marry somebody because they were just like John.' And I think she was right, it wouldn't have done. Our life's just gone on from there, and we've been married forty-odd years now. It's been a good marriage. And we have a very good family, and we've settled happily here in Somerset. And that's the end of it. Well, nearly the end of it. We're both eighty this year. But we hope to go on for a little bit longer.

Rosalind Balcon lives in Chard, Somerset with her husband, Mike Balcon.

John Hennessey today.

FIVE

A STOLEN CHILD: JOHN HENNESSEY

After the excitement was over then the hard bit came along. I will never forget it. They took the boys and girls different ways. The boys went with the Christian Brothers and the girls went with the nuns. But some of them were brothers and sisters. Some of the boys never saw their sisters again, from that day onwards.

My mother May had me out of wedlock, that was 1936. In Ireland in those days the church was so powerful that if you were born out of wedlock that was a mortal sin. So mum was practically banished from Ireland. She had to come to Cheltenham in England to have me, and it's quite obvious she had quite a struggle. And she thought she'd do the right thing, she saw the nuns, and the nuns told her: 'Well, May, this child is not yours. This child belongs to us – it's a child of God.'

Now, looking back, can you imagine this young mother? Her child was wrenched from her – and I use that word deliberately – under the pretext that this wasn't her child. So from a young baby I was with the nuns in the Sisters of Nazareth orphanage in Bristol, till I was ten. My mother told me she often visited the orphanage to see me, but the nuns discouraged her from visiting me, and when I was about four they told her that I had been adopted by a good English family. My mother had signed no papers, nothing. What she must have gone through must have been horrendous. And it was all done in the name of religion.

Now we had some old battleaxes, you know, crudely to say – but there was a few nice nuns. They fed us well, they clothed us well – I couldn't say that it was harsh. What was a macabre thing was that if a nun died, she'd be placed in an open coffin in the chapel and we had to go up and view the nun. And as children, I look back and I think – why? And the nuns used to lift us up, 'cause

When John Hennessey's mother was forced to give him up, he was put in Nazareth House orphanage in Sneyd Park in Bristol. John stayed there throughout the Second World War, and remembers, 'The sky was black with planes.'

some of us were very small, used to lift us up so we could see the nun that died. But the Mother Superior she had a tradition that when your birthday came around she'd always invite you round, you know, to the private quarters. She always used to give us a bag of lollies or sweets and give us a little present, you know? I think at this stage of my innocence I thought the nuns were my mother, 'cause they were doing the things that I expected a lady to do, you know? I think psychologically we believed that our parents were killed during the war and that's why we were in these orphanages. Because I still remember the blitz and the Bristol bombers. We used to look out the window of the orphanage and see the sky black with planes. I still remember that vividly. Just hundreds of 'em. I think that's where the story came from we were orphans.

I was about ten at this time and the nuns assembled us, you know, and they said there's some visitors coming from Australia to see you this day. We were dressed up in our Sunday best, our little suits and what have you, and these three Christian Brothers – they were in black, long robes with the white collar. They told us stories about how in Australia kangaroos would take us to school, and there was fruit everywhere, and sunshine, what have you. Well, we were only young kids, y'know, and that was like Father Christmas coming back again. And of course we had no idea where Australia was. We thought it was just round the corner. And they asked us to put our hands up, the ones that wanted to go to Australia. Well, there was about half of us put our hands up but that made no difference. We all went anyway.

A few weeks after, the nuns packed us up and we went to Tilbury docks. We had our little cases and what have you. It was quite exciting, you know: 'Aw, look at this big ship!'

I was on the first ship out to Australia after the war. We were on that ship for seven weeks believe it or not, and I think they must be the seven best weeks I had in me life, 'cause we had a ball. The nuns were supposed to have got us for school for five days a week on the ship, but when we see the nuns on the deck we used to run, and the stewards used to hide us. They were good to us, you know, they knew we were orphans. We never ever saw any school. There was about fifty of us, boys and girls. And we ended up at Fremantle, that's in Western Australia, in 1947. I can still remember it was a stinkin' hot day. We were all dressed in our suits, and there was a band playing on the wharf. At this stage we were still excited. We thought, 'Woooo, what's going on 'ere?', you know? And they took us to a big hall and we had a dinner. We felt there was something going on, but we were still excited.

Then this Archbishop came to the front of the hall with Australia's first Migration Minister. I still remember the Archbishop saying, 'Welcome, boys and girls, to Australia – we're delighted to have you because we want to populate Australia with white children, because we are frightened of the Asian hordes.' Little did we know that we were part of the White Australia policy. Fancy using innocent children to carry out a dreadful policy. After the excitement was over then the hard bit came along. I will never forget it. They took the boys and girls different ways. The boys went with the Brothers and the girls went with the nuns. But some of them were brothers and sisters. And the screaming. I can still, still hear it today. Some of the boys never saw their sisters again, from that day onwards. And vice versa.

We were taken up in an open truck to a place called Boystown Bindoon, ninety miles north of Perth. Seventeen thousand acres. We were paraded in front of these Brothers, and in front of the boys that were already there. The Brother Superior was a big white-haired Christian Brother from Ireland, called Brother Keaney. Six foot three, about seventeen stone – he was a very big, powerful man. He told us: 'Well! We're going to make men out of you. You're not going to grow up as little girls, we'll make men out of you.' And they took our little suits off us, and our little cases with our little toys and what have you. Gave us khaki shirts an' short pants – no underwear. We never saw those suits again. Never saw those toys again. We had to build this Boystown Bindoon home, 'cause when we got there, we had no toilet facilities, no bedroom facilities, no dining room facilities. We used to sleep on open verandas, concrete floors, the rain used to sweep across yer bed, and if you got wet, well, that was a bit of bad luck. We used to be on the building sites. Could you imagine, boys as young as ten, eleven, twelve on three-storey building sites, mixing lime and mortar and sand – for building. Now if you know what lime does to your skin, you'd have some idea. And we'd mix this lime and we'd be standing in it with our bare feet and of course it would burn our skin. Also, the Australian bush land in the summer can be very, very hot. Flies, the searing heat. And here we are come from England, very pale skin. It was nothing to be sunburnt. But if you complained, the Brothers would whack you over the head and say, 'Aw, you little girl, you just put up with it.' In the wintertime, the frost would be that thick on the grass and you must remember we still had no underwear, all we had was a jumper over the khaki shirt. No shoes for seven years. No shoes or boots for seven years. And we used to walk in the fields and the paddocks, and you'd look down at yer feet and there'd be blood pouring from you, but you couldn't feel it, 'cause yer feet were frozen.

And there's a stutter I've got here and that was brought about when I was about twelve. One Sunday, we were hungry, which was nothing unusual, so I got a group of the lads and we went down to the vineyard. There's nothing nicer than stolen fruit! And we got stuck into these grapes. Anyway, on the Monday morning the Brothers had been to church as they normally do, and this Brother Keaney, he was the Brother Superior, he came into the dining room, and he was in a rage.

'Hennessey!'

Opposite: Children being taken to Australia as orphans wave at the camera and at the promise of a new l abroad. The practice of sending orphans or destitute children to the outposts of the British Empire dates ba nearly 400 years, since when hundreds of thousands of children have been transported to Australia, Cana New Zealand and sometimes South Africa and Zimbabwe. The consequences for the children were serio Apart from being wrenched from their parents and siblings, who were often still alive, and from fami surroundings, the children often had to endure harsh conditions in church-run orphanages where they w used as cheap labour. Sadly, John Hennessey's story is not exceptional. By 1967, when a final boatload ninety boys and girls sailed from Southampton to Australia, as many as 150,000 children had been shipp off to a new and uncertain life abroad; sadly, the only reason that the practice stopped was that they h simply run out of children to send. In the 1980s Margaret Humphreys, a social worker from Nottingham, up the Child Migrant Trust, and the furore resulting from her work and the moving spectacle of ch migrants telling their story on television prompted questions in Parliament. Through the work of the tr many 'orphans' have been able to trace the parents they were denied, but for many it was too late.

Oh, at this time I was trembling. And he said: 'They tell me you were the leader of the group of lads that went down to the vineyard yesterday – why'd you go there?'

'I was hungry!'

And bang! He had this walking stick with a lead end to it, and he nearly flogged me to death, stripped me naked and nearly flogged me to death, and when he was finished with his big boot he kicked me out of the dining room, y'know? What was going through me mind was: 'This man's supposed to be my father – what's he doing?' I was trying to get this cured, you know, the stutter. The medical people said: John, your voice will go to the grave with you, because you will never ever forget that.

I've got to be blunt to you. We were mentally, physically and sexually abused. The Brothers were devious in that they'd put boy against boy, and you didn't know who to trust. Now, when you think that they put children against children in an orphanage, how low can you get? I still remember when I got a bit older, one of the young boys came to me and said: 'John, one of the Brothers has been playing around with me.'

That rang alarm bells. So I brought him with me down to the head Brother's office, he was sat behind this big table. I said, 'Tommy wants to tell you something.' Anyway, Tommy was only halfway through this story and this guy gets in a rage. He belts us out – with this walking stick again – he belts us out of the office: 'I don't want to ever hear a story like that again!' People have often

Brother Keaney, head of the Christian Brothers who ran the Boystown Bindoon orphanage near Perth, where John Hennessey was sent in 1947. Former child migrants are campaigning for his statue, which now stands outside the orphanage, to be taken down.

said, John why didn't you tell people this was going on? How could we, when the head of the orphanage didn't want to know about it? And I've said, come on, who would believe children? Who ever questioned the bishop, the priests, in those days? They were above the law. Some people would class us as very ungrateful children. Look at these Brothers – they fed you, they gave you a new lease of life. So who was gonna believe us? A couple of boys did escape, but there was farms around the place, and the farmers were friends of the Brothers, and all they did they picked up the boys and brought them back in again. You've gotta realise the vastness of the Australian countryside.

And the thing that hurt us most was that we thought that these people were our family, we didn't know any different, and why would your own family do that to you? They were single men, these Christian Brothers. They took a vow of chastity and all this other stuff. They despised women – they were taught that. And they told us from the time we were twelve to about eighteen that the opposite sex were evil people. Now, with a young boy that's the most vulnerable time of yer life, where yer whole body is changing, and you're being taught that the opposite sex is no good. Love to them was a dirty word and tenderness never existed. From the time I left the nuns until I think I was twenty-three – I was never cuddled. And that happened to all of us. Now, that has to have an effect on you.

I left Bindoon and took on an apprenticeship as a painter and decorator. And I was terrified in talking to young girls and young ladies and what have you, 'cause I thought I was a second-class citizen. I used to walk the streets of Perth, and for three months, I used to look at the footpath. Never used to look straight forward at people, that's how you felt. I eventually found a girl and I lived with her for six years, but I was never comfortable. I thought everything was working out until I found out she was two-timing me. Well, if you'd been through what we'd been through as children, to be once again let down, this was the last straw, and I think that's why today I stay single. But I thought – these bastards. Pardon the language, but I mean it. These bastards were determined to think that we weren't going to make a go of life. And I had an instinct in me I'd prove to them that if we're given the same rights and opportunities as other people, we could be up there with the best. So the community was my family and I didn't like injustices being done to anybody. Particularly children. I stood for council in a town outside Sydney, a population of a 150,000. Half the population under twenty-one, huge problems but huge opportunities. But over the years, I seem to have connected with the younger people, and I ended up being the Deputy Mayor, held the balance of power. And didn't talk about things, I got them done.

The reunion with my mother is – if it wasn't so sorrowful, it's a fairy tale. A wonderful woman came on the scene thirteen years ago, called Margaret Humphreys. She's the international director of the Child Migrant Trust in Nottingham. In my case, I approached Margaret and I'll be quite honest, I thought the scent had gone, how could you find my mother at this late stage in life? But not Margaret. She goes to Belfast, to look at the files. She came close many times to finding what we thought was my mother. Almost 99.9 per cent with one family. But Margaret in her wisdom said she thought we should have a blood sample. They had the blood test and it proved negative. Then she goes to Ireland and she found 145 May/Mary Hennesseys. Can you imagine? One of them had to be my mother. She whittled it down. She came across a woman, and knowing a bit about my background she asked her to verify it. She verified everything that Margaret said. And so we found out that my mother was in Ireland.

When I met my mother five years ago she looks at me in the eyes and she was trembling, she had the guilt complex. She thought I was coming to kill her! She looks at me in the eyes and she says, 'Michael John, where have you been all these years?' I'm sixty-six now, and my mother was only found five years ago. We celebrated her ninetieth birthday the other day. The first birthday card I ever got in my life was from my mother, and that was five years ago. I never ever thought I would see that card, and that's a card I treasure. To meet your own flesh and blood, when you practically were prepared to go to the grave, knowing you'd never meet your mother again. It's just unbelievable. I am one of the lucky ones. I know some of the lads flew over from Australia, not to see their mothers, but to bury them. Terrible.

There was 10,000 others that was shipped out almost secretly, unbeknown to the British people, sanctioned by Buckingham Palace, sanctioned by the

John reunited with his mother in 1997, after a lifetime apart.

For a Special Son

Happy Birthday
FROM : MUM ● DAD
          KELLY
          GOD BLESS
MICHAEL JOHN PATRICK
          HENNESSY.

John Hennessey's most
treasured possession:
'the first birthday card I ever
got in my life was from my
mother, and that was
five years ago.'

government, sanctioned by the charities and sanctioned by the churches. England, being one of the only countries in the world that ever shipped her children, her flesh and blood, and then abandoned them. Abandoned them. But the suffering, and the hurt and the deception that that act done not only to the 10,000 migrant children but to their families. Can you imagine? I could honestly say I would never want my childhood days back again, never.

John Hennessey was awarded the Order of Australia for his work within the community, but particularly for his work with the survivors and relatives of the Granville Train Disaster, the biggest rail disaster in Australia's history. He is sixty-six and lives near Sydney, Australia.

Rosa Hui today.

SIX

LEAVING HONG KONG: ROSA HUI

The first thing I noticed about Bristol is loads and loads of churches everywhere. I just couldn't understand why there were so many churches!

I was born in China in 1944. We had a huge house which occupied the whole street more or less and we divided it into different wings. We had a courtyard and from one side of the house, sometimes it takes fifteen minutes to walk to the other side of the house. In my family we have ten sisters and brothers, I'm the seventh one. My father's got an import and export business, and then he had branches all over China, especially in the south of China. The year before the Communists came and took over the country, marching down from the north, we already had a tip-off to get out of the country. Because at the time we are very well off, and we'd be regarded as landlords, and that is against Communist policy.

We escaped to Hong Kong. The population, the majority of them, are Cantonese, even though it is a British colony. And they're very hostile to people from the north, especially the rich people like us. I was only about two or three, I remember very little of it, but I do remember when I was a little girl I used to go out with servants, and we'd get stones thrown at us and we were called Shanghainese. Cantonese do not like Shanghainese, because they are thought to be very pompous! At the time we didn't think we were going to settle in Hong Kong for long. But we were told our property was confiscated by the Chinese government. If we go back to China, we will get persecuted, so we didn't go back and we stay in Hong Kong. If we go back, we'll be put in jail, even face the death penalty. I do know that later one of my uncles was enticed back, because they said, 'You come back, everything's forgiven.' And when he went back he was

Hong Kong's Queens Road in 1903 and 1920 respectively. Colonised by the British in 1841, it was extended by a 99-year lease of land from China in 1898. It became a hugely important trading centre, and after 1945 its population was swelled by an influx of war refugees and Shanghai families like Rosa's, who were fleeing China after the 1949 Communist revolution.

locked up in jail and he was sent to the field to work. He never work in his life, so he wouldn't know anything about working, and that kill him.

In Chinese culture, daughters are regarded as a bad investment. Because when they grow up and get married, they become somebody else's daughter. Daughters married to somebody else's family end up looking after the parents-in-law. Sons are the one ends up looking after the actual parents. Also because the daughters are not regarded as breadwinners, so traditionally the more sons you have the wealthier you are. That is very traditional Chinese culture. So I had a very lonely childhood, I always felt rather unwanted. I was never short of material things. I have my own dressmaker come to the house to measure me, and I also had my own hairdresser as well, and I'd go to the hairdresser once a week – but somehow, I just didn't feel there was any warmth. I felt my mother tended to favour the boys. Whenever there was something to be dished out like Chinese sausage, my mum will give one to each of the boys, but I'm the one always left without. As far as my father's concerned, he was busy making money, a businessman and all this. But my mum was a typical Chinese rich wife, and she didn't get up until after lunch, and then after that she will get herself ready, go out and socialise with other rich women, play Mah-Jong in hotels, restaurants, places like that. I'm just being left alone sitting with my servants in the servants' quarter. I was very often criticized by my mum that I shouldn't spend so much time with the servants and yet, they treated me as a human being. They actually look after me very well and I felt closer to the servants than I would be with my own parents. Which I find rather sad. But that's the way it goes, you know, the Chinese culture.

In those days we all had nannies and wet nurses, because it was traditional. The rich wives did not feed their own babies, so we employed women who served as wet nurse to all the newborn babies. But before I was born I had three sisters. My grandfather was a traditional Chinese man and he didn't want to employ wet nurses or nannies for those newborn babies. And two of them actually died because my mum wasn't feeding the babies. I don't think it's deliberate. My mother was just a victim of the culture of discrimination against girls. I know she was very much discriminated against by my family, my father's family. When she was seventeen, she produced three daughters. Therefore, with my grandparents, she was not a favourite where they were concerned. Especially after three girls, she was accused that she couldn't produce a son for the family. But when she had my eldest brother there was a big party thrown and there were firecrackers and everybody in the family business was given a day off. And instead of one wet nurse there were two, for my brother. That tells you a lot, you know, about the differences between boys and girls. Being a little girl I felt very lonely. My sister told me that Chinese girls are actually born to be tough, we got no choice, we have to prove ourselves. It's only afterwards, I prove I can live without them, I didn't need their help and I can survive and find my own way.

I think I was about seventeen when I first met my husband. I was still at school. I was educated in one of the Catholic convents, it's all girls. The family always forbid us to go out with boys, so we had to go and organise parties and invite friends or brothers or cousins who study in the boys' school. We told our family we just went to our friend to do some studies, we dare not tell our family. To meet boys at parties, that's forbidden, taboo, you know. So my husband came along to the party – that's how we met. And he asked me to dance. Then he started phoning me and asking me to go out. Even phoning has got to be very secretive as well! And I think all of a sudden I felt like I was being treated like a queen, and I was wanted by another human being. I was very young and also Chinese girls, even when we are eighteen, are very immature. But there's no way I can tell my parents that somebody's chasing after me, that there's a young man who's interested in your daughter. Firstly, he comes from a very poor family, secondly he definitely wasn't educated as well as I was, and thirdly I know my parents wanted to send me to America and they didn't want me to get involved with any boys. They wanted me actually to befriend the son of the family's friends, who were actually quite well off, and then go to America, perhaps, be near him. They wanted me married to that family, but of course it didn't work out the way they'd planned.

So I didn't take this man to meet my family. But then one day he was just waiting for me outside where I live, and we were found out accidentally by my mother. At the time my mum didn't really have a lot of time for me, but when it comes to boys, she wants to know. Whether they come from decent family, if they come from the same class, same kind of education, background, everything. If it's not better, it gotta be at least equivalent. But when I was courted by this boyfriend, he fell in love with me and then he asked me to marry him because he was offered a job in this country. I went to my parents to say instead of going to university I want to marry this young man, and my father more or less said, 'Over my dead body.' He said, 'You never even go to the kitchen to do any cooking, you don't know anything about housework, how is he going to support you? What has he got to show, how dare he ask for your hand?' A lot of unkind things were being said. Eventually, my father actually broke down and cried. And I only saw him cry a few times in my whole life. I think that was the first time I realised my father truly did love me.

Rosa made her first communion at her convent school in Hong Kong. 'I was educated in one of the Catholic convents, it's all girls. The family always forbid us to go out with boys, so we had to go and organise parties secretly.'

Rosa in 1961.

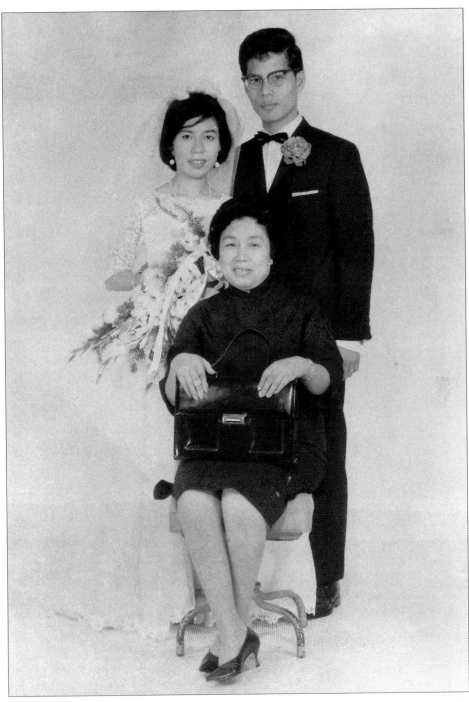

Rosa married against her parents' wishes when she was only nineteen, in 1963. She had a distant relationship with her very traditional Chinese parents, although her mother had herself endured great hardship because her first three children were girls, when Chinese tradition valued only boys.

I felt guilty. I felt I was an unworthy daughter. I felt like I was disobeying my father, I was letting him down. But yet the other side of me was dying to escape, to be loved. I wanted to be treated as a human person. My father was persuaded by my sister and her husband to give me permission to marry against his will. He was more or less forced to go to the wedding because I was under-age, and reluctantly he signed his name on the dotted line. But he refused to come to the reception because he did not agree to the marriage. And then because perhaps they really want to see the backside of me, they actually financially helped me to come to Britain. My husband came to Bristol before I did, because of his job, and I came afterwards. It was the 3rd March I left Hong Kong in 1964, so I got here on the 4th March. I wasn't sure I'd made the right decision then, but even so I made my bed I got to lie in it. I didn't like this country at all. I didn't like the cold, and I just couldn't keep warm. I put on all the clothes I could find to keep myself warm. And the first thing I noticed about Bristol is loads and loads of churches everywhere. I just couldn't understand why there were so many churches! England was very dull at the time, and unlike Hong Kong, which was always full of people and hustle and bustle, shops open until ten. Here, after five or six everything's gone dead, Sundays especially.

Rosa came from a wealthy and very traditional Chinese family, seen here in the 1960s after Rosa had gone to England. Rosa's father sits on the far left, and her mother is second from the right.

My husband got a job with one of the Chinese restaurants as a waiter. We were poor. During the day he'd go to work and I was trying to go to college and study. And of course, all of a sudden I have to grow up, I've got no servants to do my housework for me. I was trying to prove to my husband I could be a good wife. We live in one of those places, a top floor flat in Clifton, because we didn't have a lot of money and I was determined not to ask my father for help. In order to prove to my husband that I can learn and be a good wife, I start trying to cook. The next thing I know, I burned all my eyelashes and eyebrows trying to light the cooker! I burnt everything, almost my hair! So that was quite hilarious, looking back. And we had to take turns to wash the landing, and I'd never washed anything in my whole life. All of a sudden I had to wash the landing! I kept at it for about three hours on my knees, and I was still covered with suds and foam. Just couldn't get it clean. I started crying. By the time I got up from the floor, I found my knees had started to bleed, you know. All of a sudden I realised I was useless, I was really as bad as my Dad said I was. I'd been spoilt rotten. I remember when I was little girl, I went out, I had to pick the dresses from the wardrobe, and then my bed was covered with clothes and I just leave it, and by the time I come back everything was tidy. I no longer had that kind of luxury. I cried every day.

Six months after we got married, I realised I was actually expecting the first child. Things were already difficult between my husband and I then. I did begin to wonder whether I was doing the right thing, but my husband – who has done nothing wrong, it was me who made the wrong choice, that's all – I believe he truly loved me, he definitely loved me then. I was very immature and I was very much relying on my husband. I'm so used to him organising everything because that's the environment I come from. Because of my background, it's easy for me to say, you decide. I created a situation that everything was decided by my husband, and I think I got into the habit and I became submissive. But deep down inside I am not a submissive person, which I didn't know until later on, when I resented his arranging my life.

I started to work in an English environment, and my eyes begin to open. I was told that I was beginning to behave like an English woman, forgetting my place. But I began to see the other side of it, that I'm a free person and that I have my own thinking. I shouldn't do everything just because my husband says so. I have changed tremendously, from an eighteen-year-old woman coming from Hong Kong, didn't know anything, didn't even know how to cook. I begin to develop into a more mature person and I came out to work, I earn my own money.

Moving to Bristol in the 1960s was a massive shock for Rosa, who had never cooked or cleaned in her life.

But our tradition, whatever you do, the children come first, you will never ever get a divorce, and let the child suffer without the father or a mother. Chinese people who come from a good family will not even dream of having divorce in their family. And so things carried on for years, and Bristol became my home. I did walk out a couple of times, with a suitcase, standing at the bus stop, waiting for the bus to come. That was a Sunday, tipping down with rain. I walked out, and of course I chose the wrong day, buses don't run very often on a Sunday. And finally my children came and took me back to the house. Every time I wanted to leave, I looked at my two innocent children and I just couldn't do it. But things just got worse and worse, and I waited for sixteen years until my children grow up before I get my divorce, because I don't want my children to suffer.

Rosa with her father and mother.

But at the same time, I got involved with the Chinese Women's Group in Bristol. I had been working as a trade consultant on an international basis, and when I was asked to run the Chinese Women's Group, I turned my nose up, partly because I don't have anything in common with the Chinese community in Bristol, I'm virtually an outsider being from Hong Kong. A foreigner as far as they're concerned. But in the end, I got involved. There were three things about me which is taboo to them – I'm a divorced woman; two, I'm not Cantonese, that's also taboo; three, I am actually very outspoken, and Chinese tend not to favour that. I like people to be straight. Even culturally, if they don't like something, they don't tell people to their face. I think it's because I was educated in the Italian convent, and most of my classmates are foreigners. So it took me about five years to win the community, which I eventually learned to get my head down, not to say anything, just to prove myself to them. And now if there's a problem, they come to me, and I can help. And that's very important to me, very special.

Today I clash a bit with my daughter. Very often I blame myself for it because she's always been the apple of her father's eyes, and all of sudden because I asked for a divorce, I feel guilty for depriving her of a father. I'm closer to my

Traditionally, women have very few rights in Chinese society, and this continued to be the case in Hong Kong when it was part of the British Empire. This is an earlier photograph of Chinese girls in Hong Kong, probably about 1920, with their Amah or nurse.

In 2003 Rosa received the Lord Mayor's Medal for her work with the Chinese Women's Group in Bristol. She is seen here with Bristol's Lord Mayor and HTV presenter Cherie Eugene.

own mother now, but I do feel sorry for my mum. Looking back, it was definitely an escape, to come here. So today I do not blame my husband for the divorce. He came along and rescued me, in a way, from my situation at home. I think we all make mistakes when we are young, we think we know what we are doing.

Rosa Hui lives in Bristol.

Alice Harper today.

SEVEN

A MARRIAGE IN MALAYA: ALICE HARPER

My mum decided to get a charm from the Buddhist monk, and this is a special charm that looks after soldiers and makes them invisible. My husband had that in his top pocket all the time and he believed in it. And that is half the story – when you believe in something it works for you.

I was born in Kuala Lumpur, in Malaya, in 1932. I lived on a rubber plantation with my parents. Because we were the only British house, and the only other British planter was miles away, my only playmates were the rubber-tapper's children, and contractor's children. About once a month, we would go into Kuala Lumpur, and we would walk, mum and I, through a very narrow jungle. And remember this is in the thirties. It was a really jungly, narrow track. Accompanied by two Tamil tappers with big sticks, to ward off – this is not untrue, this is true – to ward off tigers. Yeah. Or mad elephants, or whatever that was going around. To me it was all a lovely game, you see. So we'd have to walk about twenty minutes down to the railway track, catch a train, go to Kuala Lumpur for a week or so. That was the highlight.

My father was one of five children, and they lived in Montrose in Scotland and they had a big farm. And then in 1929, something like that, when there was this big recession, and they lost the farm, so they sent all sons out to all of the empire. Some went to Australia, some went to India, some went to Canada. My father ended up in Malaya. In fact, he was underage, he was nineteen, but it said he was twenty-one on his passport. They all had to go out, all the sons, to make money to send money back for them to get the farm back. My dad's life was a little bit hard because he had to be on the plantation at five in the morning. He had to go and check that all the labourers were there, cutting the rubber tree. You know, they make this slit in a v-shape, and then they leave a little cup underneath to collect all the milky stuff. He was in charge of acres and acres, he was the manager.

But he loved it; that was his life. And it was like being on the farm again. Most of the planters had local wives because British women did not want to go and live on a plantation, which was very primitive in those days. You know, you had no electricity, water had to be carried in by the water carrier, 'cause you used to have a water carrier man, the gardener, the cook, and – well, you needed someone to help you.

My mum is Burmese. She was born in Thailand. She decided that there were lots of white men in Malaya, I'll go to Malaya. So she went to Malaya, met my dad, and that was it. The planters had a good time if they had a local lady or wife. If not, the planters just drank, and that's what they did because it was very boring, very hot work. And the only highlight was when they went down into town once a month or when it was St Andrew's day – 'cause most of them were Scottish, and when they went into town they really lived it up and were fighting with each other, really! Having a good old bash with each other.

Once a year the Tamils had their festivals. Everyone had a day off. When that happened my father was very happy, because he'd be sat on top of the steps just like the king, and all these labourers would be in a line, and one by one they would climb up these stairs, get to the top, kiss his feet and give him a bundle of whatever wrapped up in a cloth. It could be absolute rubbish, or it could be food or drink. And so they went on. And it took hours, but each one wanted to do it, but it was like their pride and joy that they have to pay homage to this man. So he really enjoyed that, and I did because sometimes there were things that I could play with. There were about 120 Tamil labourers, and a handful of Chinese contractors who had to maintain the huts and do all the more important jobs. They were very poor really, didn't have a lot of money. So by giving my dad these things every year, it was a big hole for them. But they wanted to do it. And sometimes in the evening dad would be sitting there, looking at a sunset, having his whisky or what-not. There'd be a big commotion, the labours calling 'Tuan'. Tuan means like boss – 'Tuan, tuan, come help!' There'd be huge boa-constrictor, huge snakes, either in the house, or outside or whatever. My dad went and shot it, and dad would skin the snake, pin the skin onto the door of this huge shed for it to dry. And I had so many snake-skin shoes, belts, and so did my dad. Mum and I would go to Kuala Lumpur, in town, and get shoes made from this skin. And then we used to get

Alice Harper grew up in Malaya on the rubber plantations outside Kuala Lumpur in the 1930s.

Monitor lizards – huge lizards, which would come on to your roof. 'Cause we had like a half atap roof. Atap is like thatch, it's coconut leaves, and half would be zinc. So if he was on the atap half it was fine, but if he was on the zinc he'd make a big row. Me being little, I was terrified of it because it had this long tongue! That was the only thing I was terrified of on that plantation.

So life for me was happy, I lived like that till I was five, and then of course I was properly put into the convent boarding school, at the age of five, which is very young, but that's what was the norm, that's what people did. The nuns, most of them were Irish, and they were really, really cruel. We didn't like it at all. But then we were invaded by the Japanese in 1942, and the war started.

Alice's mother came from Burma. 'She decided that there were lots of white men in Malaya, I'll go to Malaya.' So she went to Malaya, met my Dad, and that was it!' It was common for planters to marry non-British girls although these marriages would have been frowned on in other parts of the British Empire such as India.

Because the only other British family lived miles away, Alice's best friends were the rubber-tapper's children, seen here in 1934 (Alice is on the left).

My father was called up as a volunteer; all the British planters had to be volunteers. They all ended up in Singapore, because they thought Singapore wouldn't fall, which of course it did. We went to KL [Kuala Lumpur]. And KL was without law really, there was a lot of looting and all sort of things. So it was a bit scary. And one evening we were just sat outside on our veranda, and mum looked up, and she saw loads of men riding bicycles, you know, with their head down. And my aunt said, 'Ooh, look, at last, the Chinese have come to help the British!' And we were sort of almost going to stand up and clap when another row of cyclists came and they had a Japanese flag flying. So we thought – Oh God. But they didn't stop, they just rode along, I don't know where they were going. And then we started getting scary stories about children who were English or half being bayoneted, you see. So my mum hid us beneath the steps for three weeks.

During the war my father was a prisoner of war in Changi prisoner of war camp for three and a half years. A lot of people don't survive after they'd been in Changi. He was lucky because – well, lucky or unlucky, depending on how you look at it – because he had beriberi. And beriberi is a disease that bloats you up. So he was not sent to the Thai–Burmese railway to build the railway. But all his assistants went, all of them died. He was saved because he had beriberi. But to punish him they tied him to his chair for months on end. The only time they let him out was to go to the loo. And he survived the war. By this time we were teenagers, we don't live on the plantation any more. We went to him for the weekend from school. Electricity and water hadn't come back yet, this is just after the war. We had to have paraffin lights. Moths gather all around them, so my sister and I – I was thirteen, she was eleven – we were playing about with the moths. And we caught them, and we killed them. And I've never seen my father lose his temper as he did with us. 'Why are you killing innocent things? I've had to eat those things! Here you are, killing them willy-nilly.' He was really upset. And it was the first time I've seen my dad upset. My father was six foot two, big fellow, and he'd lost weight, he lost his get up and go. He just wanted a quiet life from day to day. It wasn't just him, a lot of them were like that, they didn't last very long. Apart from the moth incident, he never wanted to talk about his time in prison. He just said, it's horrible.

And then things didn't get any better. After the war, the Chinese Communists started a guerrilla war because they wanted to take control of the country. They were killing people. When I was little, all dad's plantations were right out in the jungle, which is now our national park, right in the middle of Malaya. But as he got a bit older they gave him plantations just out of town. But the Communists just wanted them out, the British, and then they gave a price for his head to the villagers. To his own Tamil labourers. To kill him. It was easier than them coming to kill him, you see. And the first thing we knew about it all these posters were up. Just on trees, and post offices, with his face. It was directed towards the labourers and the villagers. Just to inform them when my father was in, what time he was in, where he would be, and things like that. The first planter that got killed was one of his assistants, I think his name was Stuart. They just went to the house and shot him, and his wife, and his little girl – she was about three or four. That was the first one, that's when it all started. By this time my father had a concrete bungalow – out go the wooden

…aya had been controlled by Britain since 1914, and there had been heavy investment in rubber plantations and …mines. It was seen as an important imperial asset, and thousands of men, such as Alice's father, seen here in the …0s, went out to Malaya to work on the plantations to make their fortune. It was hot, hard work, but work was …emand in the 1930s, and more than half the labourers on the plantations were either Chinese or Tamil Indians.

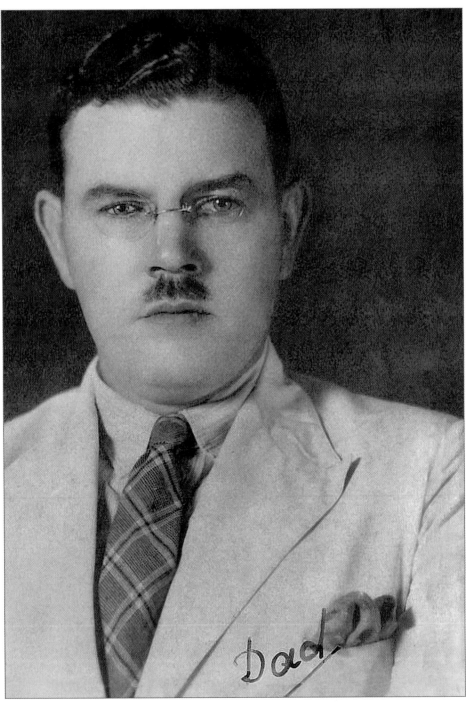

Dad.

Alice's father came from Scotland, and went to Malaya to seek his fortune after the family farming business faltered during the 1930s depression. The Scottish were to be found in the farthest flung corners of the empire, and in fact some parts of the empire were dominated by and run by Scots.

houses on stilts, we are a bit more modern now. And I remember him moving his bedroom into the middle of the house so that he had lots of rooms surrounding him. My father was very unhappy because he'd just come out of prison, and he was a nervous wreck already. And then to be told that you're being hunted. The whole estate was lit up with these huge lights, security lights. Really, really big ones. It was like being in a prisoner of war camp again.

You had to be wary about what you said, and who your friends were. We didn't say too much. British soldiers were being killed, which upset us really, but that was how it was. I was frightened for myself, I was frightened for my mum, but I was more frightened for my dad because, you know, I loved him so much. We used to go up for the weekends, but then he eventually said not to come up. He'd come and stay with us, which relaxed him a bit. We were living in the city by then, a big house on a big main road, very wide. All that road was

During the war, Alice's father was taken prisoner and endured the horrific cruelty of the Japanese-run Changi prisoner of war camp. He was deeply affected by the experience, and his health suffered badly. By 1948, when this photograph of him and his Tamil gardener was taken, the Communist uprising was in full swing in Malaya, and his life was again under threat.

quite posh, all ex-pats there, big houses. And further up, three miles away, was a big Chinese house with a big compound as they call it, which was taken over by the British army, the Royal Engineers. And they were like the maintenance people. In the evenings about six or seven o'clock, that was the time when the wind stopped and we could play badminton. We had a little makeshift badminton court at the front of the garden. My sister and I – remember, we're about fifteen, and we used to see this Royal Engineer going up and down on his Harley motorbike. And then one day we waved, and then next day he waved back. And then the next day he just stopped. And he said, 'Can I come and play badminton?' And so we said, yes, if you want to.

And so Stan came, and he played and he won the blooming thing! He was very fair. Blue, blue eyes. I like fair people. He knew it all, and he won all our badminton games. And when we played board games he would win. And he'd like to tell you how to do things in a better way, so he got on your nerves a bit! But underneath all he was very genuine, and very loving, and very caring. I did have a lot of boyfriends, and it wasn't serious, but with Stan somehow it became serious. And he used to date the two of us, my sister. We never knew who he liked! Then he had a bad motorbike accident, and his right arm was paralysed. He was the only soldier who saluted with his left hand after that. He had to come home for treatment. So in August he just asked me if I would marry him. We were in a night-club when he popped the question. I could hardly hear him because the band was so loud. I said, 'What did you say?' My sister was with me again, so it was a threesome, all the time! So we got engaged in August, married in September, so we had October at home, and in November we were on the troop ship to freezing England. And I was seventeen and a half then. I had to have my parents' permission. He was twenty-one and a half. So we got married, and it seemed it was the right thing.

But it was not a normal time and a lot of the British were thinking, we're going. Slowly but surely they sacked all the British planters, and replaced them with their own people. And it broke dad's heart really, because he was out there since he was nineteen. That was his life. And then he had a couple of heart attacks. He stuck it out, and he stuck it out, but eventually he'd had enough. So he left, came back to Montrose, and bought a little farm. And promptly died. So that was the end of him, you see. I think he would have loved to have retired there, it was like his second home. But it was not to be.

We went back a second time for the Emergency. Stan was sent out into the jungle to build all these huts for the troops that were coming. He used to go and do all the loos, all in the jungle – Stan, Stan the sanitary man, I used to call

3 September 1949 Alice married Stan, a young British soldier based in Malaya. She had to get special ⌐mission from her parents because she was only seventeen.

Alice in 1949, aged seventeen.

Stan in 1949, aged twenty-one.

Stan pictured in 1948
with Malayan colleagues.

him! Because we did not live in army quarters, 'cause Stan didn't like living in army quarters, we always rented outside the camp. And rather than go to the camp and report he used to go straight to the jungle to save time. And he used to go on his own without a convoy. That was a very worrying time for me. If they shot him, fine, but the Chinese Communists were ruthless people, they would torture you. They would string you up upside down and then start hacking you about. I told him he was not to take risks. My mum was also worried, so she decided to get a charm from the Buddhist monk, and this is a special charm that looks after soldiers, and this charm is supposed to make them invisible. It's a piece of cotton, with all sorts of writing and pictures on it. He had that in his top pocket all the time and he believed in it. And that is half the story – when you believe in something it works for you, and we've still got it today. So he survived the Emergency.

We lasted fifty-three years. We always held hands. By 2002 when we went to bed, and he had cancer, and I couldn't hug him because he was very tender, we still held hands. We were still in love, but it was more so because we knew we'd only have six months. So each day we try to make it very precious. The Malayan

Stan and Alice celebrated their golden wedding anniversary in 1999, at Portishead, Somerset.

and Borneo Veterans' Association gave him a military funeral. The place was packed. Anyway. I went back to Malaysia recently for two reasons: one was nostalgic, to see all the places that Stan and I visited. And to see if I could live there again. But as soon as I got off the plane I knew I could not live there. Portishead is my home, and I'll live and die here.

Alice Harper lives in Portishead, and is now retired. Having met Alice playing badminton, Stan founded the badminton club at Portishead sports centre, where there is now a plaque in his memory.

Alan Chidgey today.

EIGHT

WAR IN THE JUNGLE: ALAN CHIDGEY

The people that we killed was young. I thought my God, let's hope that it was one of the terrorists. I felt very, very sick inside. It's something that stays in your mind for the rest of your life because you never forget that. It's a horrible, horrible thing.

In 1953 I was called up for my National Service for two years, but I wanted to go in for seven years. I was sent to Taunton Barracks in Somerset. I went up for my medical and everything. It took me all day, and I passed A1. After that they says all right, you're ready to go in the army, so me and my mother went into this officers' room — even though I asked her to stay outside — and we had a good old yap. They said, 'I take it that you want to go in the army for seven years?' And the next minute Hell lets fire and my mother gets up behind me and she said, 'No! I don't want my son to go in the army for seven years!' She said, 'He's doing his National Service, for two years, and if he likes it after that, fair enough.' So I was really uppity you know, but he looked up, he said, 'Well, that's fair enough, just sign here please.' And the next minute, going home on the train with Mum you know in her mood, I couldn't speak to her you know. After I found out what the army life was all about, I could see what she meant.

It was hard in the army, and I was always getting into trouble. They called me 'Trouble Chidge'! In the Light Infantry, marching was 128 steps a minute — and that is fast. If you didn't march properly, you was told to get your rifle and run round the square, rifle above your heads, at least ten times. If you done it slow, you had to go round another ten times. So you had to do it at full pelt, every time. The sergeant was watching you as he put the other lads through their paces on the square, 'Move on that man, move on, I'm watching you.'

And you was absolutely shattered and you felt, 'Oh my God – I can't go on!' And then: 'Get that rifle up!' And your beds had to be squared, everything sparkling. It had to be perfect. And the sergeant would come in a couple of times with me and he looked at my bed and said, 'Hmm . . . is this the best you can do is it?' And he catches hold of the sheet and he pulls it all off the bed and he says, 'Now put it right!' So you was on a loser all the time.

Once, they confined me to barracks because of me hair. I had long hair. And I had three haircuts in two days. I had one in the morning, one in the afternoon and one the following afternoon. And every time I was inspected they kept saying to me, 'Am I standing on your hair?' And I said, 'I don't think so.' They said, 'Well, 'tis long enough!' And they'd put you on a charge for that. You had to do what they wanted you to. You know, like spud bashing or something. Make sure you take the eyes out of the potatoes and things. Well, I was eighteen years old, and I think in a way I was a little bit frightened of them, but they made a man out of me.

Then we was told we were going to Malaya. It did come as a shock. I couldn't get round to telling my mother. In the end, someone says to my mother, 'What do you think of the boys going off to Malaya?' And when I got home Mum was waiting for me, weren't she. She said, 'How's it you ain't said nothing about going to Malaya?' So I said, 'Well you know, I didn't want to get you edgy or anything like that, you know.' She was a very edgy person, you see. So she came down to Southampton, to the ship to see me off. We all had our kit bags and everything, and we was walking up the gangplank to go on board the ship, the *Empire Trooper*. My mum was very, very upset. Oh, I can see her face now. I idolised my mum, and I could feel it in myself, that sadness. She'd read in the paper about what was going on in Malaya and things like that. And I thought that would be the last time I would see my family. That's why I had a few tears.

The Malaya campaign had been going on for a long time, but it was still tough. We actually took five weeks to get to Malaya on that tub, the *Empire Trooper*, five weeks. Cramped conditions, nobody had any space. You weren't allowed to be sick over the side of the boat, because the portholes down below was always open, and the wind would blow it – well, it was one complete mess. I used to say to me mates who were being sick, 'Suffer you so-and-so!' You know, I had no sympathy. But as we hit the Bay of Biscay, the tide turned! I was really bad, really sick – I wanted to die! But eventually, we arrived at Singapore, and travelled to Kuala Lumpur, up to our camp.

We were in these companies near the jungle, and we had to go into the jungle – the rubber, as we called it. Our job was to look for the Communist insurgents,

Alan did his jungle training in Yorkshire before leaving for Malaya. Here he is sporting his new haircut. He had had much criticism about his hair previously from his superiors: 'They kept saying to me, "Am I standing on your hair?" And I said, "I don't think so." They said, "Well, 'tis long enough!"'

the terrorists. It was so hot, we sweated away. One of the things I hated most was the mosquitoes and the leeches. You'd take off your clothes and see if you could get a bit of air to your body. And you'd look down and see the leeches around your waist, and you take your boots off and you'd have black ankle socks made of leeches, and nobody don't seem to have a cigarette or any salt so I could burn 'em off. You know, to get them on your body – I literally had thousands of leeches on my body. It was terrifying to have a leech on you. You had to be on your guard every second, not every minute, every second. We used to go along with our rifles, or with me Bren gun, and we always had our safety catch off. Ready for attack. I was really frightened, and I wasn't the only one. You just didn't know what was round the corner, see. You were on patrol for weeks, looking for Communist insurgents, and you'd be wading through swamps up to your knees, just brown water like a cup of tea. There was water everywhere, and the smell was unbearable. We'd come back after a week, maybe two weeks, in the jungle and we'd have to go in front of the commanding officer. He used to stand back about six feet away from you: he couldn't get nowhere near you because of the smell. You smelt something terrible, absolutely terrible.

Alan as a young National Service recruit in 1952.

But the sense of humour was good. It kept you going. We used to tie our hammocks – bashers, we called them – between two trees. And the thing is, you had to get in this tree without getting your dry suit wet. Our dry suit was the dry set of clothes we carried with us, because we were always getting wet in the jungle. So this particular day I was getting changed for the night, sitting in my hammock doing well, and then all of a sudden over went the hammock. I had me dry suit on, didn't I. So I had to sleep in a new wet suit – not very nice. But I heard a few voices saying, 'Serve you blinking right, see what you're doing next time!' A little bit of morale like that, see, used to keep you going.

My mother fought on. She kept sending me letters and parcels, and she'd send cake. Mum used to make a lovely cake, a beautiful cake. The only snag was, when the parcel came through, the boys would look over and say, 'Mother's cake again Chidge! Don't forget me, mind!' and I used to say, 'Yes, you certainly will have a piece.' But when I opened it up there were ants inside. You never seen ants like it in your whole life! How the ants got in there I don't know! There was millions of them! So I says, 'There's only one place for this – straight in the bin!' It was a shame, but we did have a laugh. I didn't tell Mother that though. What I told mother was, 'You make a lovely cake and the boys thought the world of it.'

We had a few encounters, a few contacts with the terrorists. One day we found jars of rice buried in the ground – the villagers had been giving rice to the terrorists. The police put a curfew on the village between the hours of seven o'clock in the morning and seven o'clock at night. So then we hid in ambush for these people, because we knew they'd come for the rice. We stayed there for two, three nights, and on the third night, about four o'clock, we saw these lights coming down the trail. As they got nearer you could hear Chinese talking, and all of a sudden, Hell let rip. We must've been firing for at least three or four minutes. It was deafening. I think this is what I got here now (*points to his hearing aid and laughs*).

Then everything went quiet. Even the monkeys stopped chirping. We dare not make a move because they could've been acting that they were dead, but by about eight o'clock in the morning we had to make a move. We went over, and there were about four or five villagers in the dirt track. There was one with his leg blown right off, he must've bled to death because there was no actual bullet holes in the man at all. It was one of those things. It was sad, that we might have killed an innocent person, but when they started shooting I had to follow them. The people that we killed was young. I thought my God, let's hope that it was one of the terrorists. I felt very, very sick inside. It's something that stays

Alan with other members of the Somerset Light Infantry in the early 1950s. He stands fourth from the righ on the top row.

in your mind for the rest of your life because you never forget that. It's a horrible, horrible thing.

It was the ambushes that I didn't like at all. We had to do that a lot, ambushes. We'd go off in a truck, and you had to keep your head down. If you got attacked you had to head for cover – it could be a tree or a rock. You had to return fire, and then give chase. The thing is, if you come into contact with terrorists and you kill them, you gotta bring 'em out of the jungle, so that they could be photographed and identified. They wanted to have a look at them, you know. The thing was if you were taking two days to take a body out, it didn't smell very nice.

I had a friend, a good friend. Well liked by everybody, well liked. Every time you catch him he was always cleaning his teeth! He looked after his teeth something great. We were on a training exercise in the rubber, in the jungle. We was training for ambushes. The lieutenant took us out for that day, and he was the one who was gonna ambush us. We were along in the truck and all of a sudden, 'Bang, Bang, Bang!' Truck stopped. Everybody jumped off apart from this friend – he was a little bit slow getting off, you see what I mean? I dived to a ditch and he dived for a hill. But he was slipping, and the lads tried to help him. And this officer turned the gun, and pointed it at him, and fired all around

Alan made many close friendships in the army. To this day he is still in touch with many of his old comrades.

him to warm him up more or less – to make him go a bit faster. But one of the bullets ricocheted off the side of the rock and went straight into his knee and shot up inside him. Everything stopped. We shouted, 'Somebody been hit!' We took him back into camp, and we laid him on the floor. I had his head on me knee and I said, 'Come on mate, won't be long before we is going home.' He had that smile on his face, beautiful smile he had. And he was saying, 'Oh aye, they got me this time hadn't 'em!' It was terrible to see it. He died on his way to hospital.

I cried bitterly, you know. Handkerchiefs, well – I ran out of them. His grave is still out there in Kuala Lumpur now. We went out a few years ago, and spent the whole day at his graveside. We put poppies on all the Somersets that were killed, but there was far too many to put poppies on all the rest. We put a wreath on the memorial and oh, it was sad. I still think of him now. There was eight of us – no, six of us that went. And the graves is absolutely immaculate. Really nice. And the Chinese, and those looking after their graves, were so handy – I never knew anybody so bloody friendly. They wanted to do everything for us see. 'We'll do this, we'll get you that.' I gave them some money as well – 'Keep the good work up. Look after him.' That's one thing that I'm pleased with, that I've been back and seen his grave again.

Alan Chidgey went out to Malaya with the Somerset Light Infantry, and is still involved with his local veterans' association. He is sixty-eight and lives in Bridgwater.

Roy Hackett today.

NINE

A JOURNEY ACROSS THE SEA: ROY HACKETT

We had spoken to people that were here much longer than I, to find out why they didn't do something about it. And they said, 'The Lord Will Provide.' And my words to them was, 'He will provide only when you put your shoulder to the wheel!'

I was born in Jamaica in the parish of St Mary's, in 1928, 18 September. We were poor, life was tough; my parents were very poor. We grew up in the country and we had to do everything for ourselves. My father worked the fields, what we call cultivation, and my mother just looked after four children, myself, my two brothers and my sister. My father actually worked very hard to keep us, we never wanted for anything but shoes. We just couldn't afford shoes for everybody so we just had one that we wore to church on Sundays. Going to church we just gotta go half-way then put it on. And then coming back we take it off again, because it's called Sunday best! I grew up feeling British, speaking English, and when I got older I decided to travel. And I did not want to go to the United States, which I could have done. Everybody was aimed for the United States, but I said I wanted to see Mother England, because I felt British, part of the empire. I decided when I was twenty-two that I am coming, and I just packed up and came to England. I didn't even tell my parents. I think they always think that I was, what we call 'Own Way'. Regardless what you tell me, I listen, but I never do what you says. And because of that they know that I always do things my own way. It was after I reached England I wrote my parents and told them I was in England. It was a decision I had to take for myself.

I came by boat to Liverpool. I got here 1952, 15 October. What surprised me when I came to Liverpool it was a Sunday, and I didn't know people actually worked on Sundays. And there were these blokes, white blokes, with their shirts off in October. Their shirts off on the railway, working. And I thought, Good Heavens, why they do that? Don't they know it's the Sabbath? But I got to know, and I take it as nothing to go to work on a Sunday because I got to adopt what happening here. It was wintertime in October, they were burning coal because those days there were no heating in the houses like what you have now. It was coal or coke or whatever you were burning. And there was all this smoke from the chimneys. And I thought these were factories. I didn't have anyone to tell me it wasn't. And I had that in my mind all along, for quite a while. And then I found out that the smoke was not really from factories, it was from homes burning the coal. It was exciting. I wrote home and told them about it!

Eventually, I went to London and while I was out looking for jobs, I came across Taylor Woodrow. And he asked me if I was looking for a job. I said, yes. He said, 'Would you look abroad?' I said yes, because I come from abroad. He said, 'Would you go to the country to work? Up in Somerset?' I say, 'I don't mind. Where is that, is it in England?' I was working as a teaboy in the Turbine Hall in Hinckley Point, which was Britain's first atomic power station. I loved being a teaboy, because as a matter of fact it was very cold out there, and as teaboy I could find ways of keeping warm. I had to go to the canteen with a canister and fetch the tea back to where the men were working in the turbine hall. But when in the canteen, I'm in the warm! I had to collect the jack hammer points when they get dull or broken, and take them to the blacksmith shop. And that was the best part of the job because I sat around there for hours in the warm drinking, while the men were out there dying with cold. And I could work all the overtime in the world as well.

But near to Christmas '59, I was told that I would be redundant, so I start looking around for another job. I thought I was going to be teaboy forever! I ended up stopping in Bristol. I lived in Lower Ashley Road, near to where the big roundabout is now. And there was about five to seven families living in a five-bedroom house, you know. It was not very nice. One kitchen, small kitchen, for seven families. There wasn't even a bath in the house. We had to travel all the way down to St Philip's on Saturdays – one bath day, Saturdays – to these baths. We take our towel and our soap and trot along down there, and then have a bath and come back up. We did have a washbasin at the back of the house that you could take indoors, but our room was so packed you couldn't find anywhere to put that pan even to have a bath in. It was sad.

My girlfriend decided to come over in 1957 and I started saving to send for her, it was about forty or fifty pounds for the plane at the time. I had to find a

Roy Hackett in May 1958, around the time that he first came to Bristol to work.

St Paul's was extremely run down by the end of the war, with bomb-damaged housing and deteriorating living conditions. It was a forgotten area of the city. By the 1950s some of its white population began moving out to the new housing estates away from the city centre, and immigrants moved in. But St Paul's was still a predominantly white area, even though it had soon gained an unfair reputation for black crime and prostitution.

place for us to live with a bit more space. I would go along the road to see if we could find any place where we could get a room or a flat or whatever. And there's always the card in the door to say 'No Dogs, No Gypsies, No Blacks'. And that would go on for ten houses, out of twenty on the road. And for them that didn't have a card, you ring the doorbell or knock the door, and politely ask, and they'll slam it your face. This is something that went on very frequently, as far as we are concerned. Matter of fact, it was only Asian people that always rent us places, because they were here long before us, they were established with houses, taxis and so forth. But it was horrendous for us black people and in particular Jamaicans. Anyway, my girlfriend came, and we live in one room in City Road in St Paul's. And when we were going to get married I just walked from my door into the church, because the church was number 4 and I was number 8.

I had lived in Jamaica all the time amongst white people and I never thought that I was any different from them. When I came here I did see the difference. Because I was put in my place that I was black, that I was a nigger, and many things that make me very ashamed of even being British, actually. Being born in

Paul's was a poor area of Bristol for many years, with both black and white families having to endure reme poverty, such as these children filmed by HTV in the 1960s. As the West Indian and Asian migration of the 1950s began, many graduated towards the area because the large houses could be shared ily and were therefore unusually affordable, and the cosmopolitan population of Bristolians, Poles, Italians Hungarians were comparatively friendly to the new arrivals.

Jamaica I felt British. But I was harassed, not physically, verbally. And body language tells a great deal in people, and you do pick up body language in people. I supposed they pick up my body language as well. I felt so deprived of the things I would want to do, because I was not allowed. It's like you shouldn't do this, because you're a black man. You shouldn't want to go into no office and work, because that's a white man's job. They didn't say that, but that's the impression I formed from what I was told. I felt terrible about Britain, because we were so proud of being part of the British Empire. And most people thought we came here to pick up money off the street of London. We did not. I did not expect to find money on the street. I wouldn't be stupid enough to know that money was there on the street, and people in Britain leave it there and walk about! When I came and see the kind of welcome I had, and the way people handled me, it's as if I was nothing. And when they say, 'Go back where you

Roy Hackett in 1963.

came from.' A couple of times people ask me, 'Why do you come here?' And I says, because there's too many white men in Jamaica, I gotta make room for them! And that was a joke, but at the same time I wanted to hurt them as well as they hurt me, for asking why did I come here.

In Bristol, on the street the women were a bit polite to us, but only when the men were not around. But if you had spoken to this lady today, and you had seen her tomorrow with her husband, she wouldn't speak to you at all. The men were aggressive to us, very aggressive. Matter of fact, many times we gotta walk two and three, that we don't get bashed by men. Of course, I'm a small person, and most of us were young and tiny, you know what I mean? And therefore one big white man could bash two of us at the same time! And even on the buses, I got up once to give a pregnant woman my seat, and she wouldn't sit in it. That's how bad it is. And if you're sitting in the seat, and there's a seat beside you empty, and some ladies or some gentleman come into the bus, they just wouldn't sit there, they stand up all through their journey, beside you. It's simply telling that I don't want you, I don't need you, I don't want to sit by you. It makes me feel sick inside. Why am I getting this across here, which should be the Mother Country?

We didn't believe in getting the dole – I've never, never had the dole in my life. I myself, I've always worked, but I had trouble in getting jobs sometimes. I happened to see in the *Evening Post* at the time that they wanted somebody to work at the docks. This place was down in Hotwells somewhere. It was based right outside the swinging bridge. I took a bus from St Paul's into the centre of Bristol, and then phoned these people and told them where I was, and asked them how would I get there. They told me that I could catch another bus, and then somebody else said it's just round the corner, you can walk. So I walked, and when I got there I knock at the window, and this young lady came out. She might have been the secretary. And she said, 'What can I do for you?' And I said that I just rang about ten minutes ago for the job that is vacant here. She said, 'Give me a minute', and she went back in. She was very polite to me. And she came out, and she said, 'I'm sorry the job is gone.' I said, 'But I only rang ten minutes ago! And it's gone?' And she said, 'The boss said he's given the job to somebody else.' And I had a white friend, and I asked him to ring about the job. And they said the job was still open.

Another time I went to St Anne's Board Mills and we were all queued up – names, address, whatever. They came to me, but I was the first black person there. The bloke said, 'Oh sorry, we don't employ Africans.' I said, 'I'm glad, I'm Jamaican.' Then he didn't know what to do. His face turned really, really white as a sheet. When he said he didn't employ Africans I know exactly what he wanted to say. But he was not brave enough to say that he don't employ black people. I said, 'Why don't you tell me that you don't employ black people?' But give him his due, he took my name and address and he sent me away. I wrote a letter, and I got a reply back that the job was vacant. And I went back and I had the job.

We did process work. They had thing that made the paper, it comes from a block, and that comes up the River Avon on barges on to St Anne's Mill, and we have to unload it by crane. I was a crane driver for about five years, and then became foreman, the first black man to do so there, because I persuaded them that I was the right man for the job. I was the foreman over fifty-two people, and I only had one black worker. All the others were white. And we get on well, because I didn't force them into anything because they were there longer than me and they do their jobs. So I didn't have a lot to tell them to do, because they knew what they were doing.

I did once have to sack someone on Christmas Eve because he hadn't turned out for three days, and he knew the drill, that you have to take a doctor's certificate. And he didn't bother to bring one. It didn't go down too well. But you can't win them all, and everyone was working as a team, and there was no face-to-face prejudice. I did that job for twenty years until I was made redundant.

By this time I was a father, you know, a husband, a father. I actually had a house in Royte Hill and I had to pay my mortgage, I gotta feed my wife, I gotta feed my children. So I just kept working and so did my wife, with her dressmaking. Life was hard for us. I was poorly paid; up to 1963 I was only earning £20 a week, that's just pocket money to some kids. And apart from just feeding the children, I had a mortgage to pay.

We wanted things like holidays, which I just couldn't afford. So we used to go down to Severn Beach, they call it the mudflats, and they used to have some entertainment for kids down there, ice cream, rides, candyfloss, we used to take them down there on my free weekends, and we'd drive down there and come back in the evening. The women would take the kids to the beach, the men would go to the pub, sit outside, have a drink. It was great for the kids, and when we do have a little bit more money then we go down to Weston-super-Mare and spend a day. It was great at the time, there was not much around better than that.

My wife wanted to be a bus conductress. I don't know why, because she is a qualified dressmaker. But she just wanted to become a bus conductor. She rang up to find out when she could come for an interview for a job. They told her the

...y and his wife Ena with daughters Laverne (centre) and Marva (right) in 1967, the year he helped to set up St Paul's Festival.

Roy and wife Ena in a grocer's in St Paul's, 1963, talking to HTV: 'St Paul's was in this state for years an people have started to blame us, the coloured people, for doing it. But we are not to blame at all, because ; far as forty years ago the same thing was happening in St Paul's and we only started coming here abou fifteen years ago.'

day and when she went they told her that they didn't want any person at all. And we knew that was wrong, because it was always in the *Evening Post* that they don't have no drivers or conductors to run the Bristol buses. The buses were owned by the Corporation, Bristol City Council, and yet they wouldn't employ black people that were living here. It was said that the white man would not like their wife on the back of a bus, conducting, while a black man was driving it. Because at the time all buses were conducted and they were mostly women conductresses. I think the bus Corporation had a hidden policy, and they must have had sanction from the union, because the union was a powerful union and they could dictate at the time. It was sad. My wife felt very disappointed. She tell people about it, but that's as far as it goes. There was no one to complain to about it. There was no such thing like what we have now, Bristol Racial Equality Council, that you could have made complaint to.

At that time, many people went to London, Birmingham, Wolverhampton and see black people driving the buses there. And we thought that Bristol was a far smaller county and town, and why can't they have black people? And we had spoken to people that were here much longer than I, to find out why they didn't do something about it. And they said, 'The Lord Will Provide.' And my words to them was, 'He will provide only when you put your shoulder to the wheel!' We decided that something had to be done. We decided to boycott the buses. And we decided to go along the route that we wanted to boycott, which was from where Muller Road comes to Fishponds Road, down through St Paul's,

Campaign follows coloured worker bar

W. INDIANS 100 p.c.
30/4/63
FOR BUS BOYCOTT

West Indians' boycott on Bristol's buses—in protest against e Omnibus Company's refusal to recruit coloured crews—was full swing this afternoon.

to right, Audley Evans, Paul Stephenson and Owen Henry, discuss the campaign.

13-3-By KEITH CHALLEN

THE first two coloured people to be hired in Britain as traffic wardens have been engaged by the City of London police. They are both women, and are due to begin meter duties on Sunday, April 17, after two weeks' training.

Last month Mr. Roy Jenkins, the Home Secretary, said he would like to see coloured policemen in Britain's police; if there were suitable applicants. He said then : "There should not be a gap between the police force and the coloured community. I think that one move to prevent this would be if we could see a certain number of coloured faces in blue uniforms."

The move by the City of London police in recruiting coloured traffic wardens may well be paving the way to enlisting coloured policemen, in London or in other forces. There have already been coloured "specials" on duty elsewhere.

A campaign leader said "We have got 100 per cent support from the city's 7,000 West Indians.

"None of them is using buses this afternoon. Although it is hard to tell, we are sure many white people are supporting us."

All-out fight

Bristol's West Indians are asking Parliament, Bristol City Council and all Christians to support them in their "all-out fight against the ruthless racial policy" of the company.

They were today approaching the Bishop of Bristol, the Bishop of Clifton and Bristol Council of Christian Churches asking them to denounce racial discrimination in the company.

The Council of Christian Churches were meeting this afternoon, and a member said this might be on the agenda.

The campaign decision follows the refusal by the company to

MPs DEMAND TOUGHER RACE HATE LAWS

AN all-party group of angry MPs last night demanded Government action to strengthen the law against incitement to race hatred.

Their move followed an announcement in the Commons that there are not sufficient grounds to justify prosecutions in two cases raised by MPs. The MPs put down a motion urging the Government to amend the Act to ensure that adequate powers are available.

Select'd

The two coloured women were among the 30 applicants who answered an advertisement. From these, 13 women and two men were selected for training.

One woman is a West Indian in her late twenties who has lived in England for eight years. Until recently she worked as a bus conductress.

The other woman is an Anglo-Indian in her late thirties. Both are married.

Chief Supt. H. Webster told me: "in selecting persons for traffic wardens we look for intelligence, a pleasant man-

ner and the ability to carry out their duty fairly.

"It so happens that these two women fulfilled their requirements. They will get the same pay as other wardens, £790 a year.

"I see no reason why any coloured women we select should not carry out the duties of a traffic warden as well as anyone else. We are hoping that when they have completed their training they will be allowed to integrate into our force almost without notice."

A spokesman for the Automobile Association said: "We see no reason at all why coloured people should not be employed as traffic wardens.

"How will coloured people be accepted by the other wardens? These I spoke to as they patrolled City streets said that they had no objection to working alongside them.

7-1 on Labour

LADBROKES, the London bookmakers, said yesterday that £100,000 had been invested in the previous three days on a Labour win at the General Election, and the their revised prices were 7-1 on Labour and 5-1 against the Conservatives.

e *Bristol Evening Post* covered the bus boycott extensively during April 1963. It even gained national news verage and caused the Bristol Labour MP and then Trade Secretary Tony Benn to ask questions in rliament. Among the leaders were Paul Stephenson, Bill Smith and Owen Henry, and their landmark victory s seen as having hastened the new Race Relations Act of 1965.

Bristol university students joined West Indian activists and locals on the streets to protest against the fact that the Bristol Bus Company would not employ black conductors or drivers.

The bus boycott was won on 28 August 1963, when Bristol Bus Company bosses agreed to employ black and Asian conductors and drivers. This was the same day that 150,000 black and white Americans marched on Washington, the biggest ever civil rights demonstration and the day that Martin Luther King gave his 'I Have a Dream' speech. The first black bus conductor to get a job was the late Raghbir Singh, pictured here.

through City Road. We go along there, we offer some people lifts, some accept it, some don't and they took the buses. There was only about twelve of us, and we go along the road in the mornings, fortunately I did have a car, I had a Vauxhall Cresta at the time. We get a great deal of support from white women, mostly. Not a lot from white men. I can't remember any white man ever give us any word of 'Go on, do it, you're entitled to it.' But we got a lot from white women. That was fortunate for us. But I must tell you the truth. I was extremely angry. There were people who said we shouldn't do it, because we should think of the other people who they are going to throw out of their jobs.

And I always assured them that providing they haven't done anything against the law I don't think an employer is going to throw them out of their jobs. I don't think that was very comforting to them, but I do it just the same because the thing about it, it's something that has to be done, and it has to be done now. If we didn't do it when we were young, then I don't think I would have the energy to do it when I'm much older.

We went on with the boycott like this for nearly six weeks, and then we said no, we cannot waste time in trying to persuade the people. We got to persuade the authority. So we decided to blockade the bus station, which was, at the time, in Fishponds Road. And we did that for about two to three days. We understood that the union was against it. And this was a trade union. Honestly, I never thought it possible, I was a member of that union. It did affect my wife. At one time she was very, very scared. Because she was carrying my last daughter Laverne at the time, she was very scared about it. And she thought, why don't you drop this thing, you're gonna let people throw stones through the window. I said no, no. My words were that some got to suffer for some to survive. I suppose being a lady and having children, I think she thinks quite different from me. I wanted to do what I think was right. The blockade went on and on until about two weeks later we decided that we did enough, let's go and sit down and talk with them. They decided to allow some of us to go on the bus. The first person after the concession was a bloke called Mr Singh, who died only recently. We felt good that we'd won, but we felt bad as well because we shouldn't have had to put a lot of people through the aggro that we had inflicted.

The Bristol West Indian Parents and Friends Association was set up in 1962, before the bus crisis. We set it up for the simple reason of helping the newcomers, because they were coming with their wives and children. We had to take them to the labour exchange, have them sign on, their wives and children had to sign on to doctors and so forth. And help them to get into schools, help them to get jobs. After the bus boycott, we decided, what can we do now? We decided to have a Jamaican-type festival. This was 1968. And we formed this festival group, which I was part of, and we pulled in Paul Stephenson and many more people that were there at the time. We draw up what we're going to do, and we come up with the wording that we will call it a West Indian Festival. Then we said, 'No, it's not only West Indians is going to profit from it, we'll call it St Paul's Festival.' So the name St Paul's Festival had been established since 1968. I think we only had about four trucks, and to us that was great, it was a beginning. Looking back on it now it wasn't so great but what can you

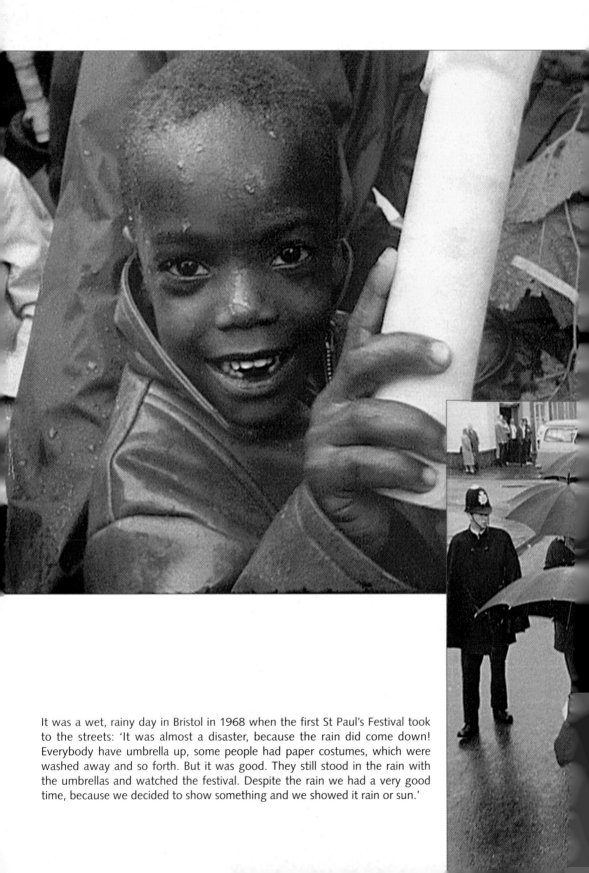

It was a wet, rainy day in Bristol in 1968 when the first St Paul's Festival took to the streets: 'It was almost a disaster, because the rain did come down! Everybody have umbrella up, some people had paper costumes, which were washed away and so forth. But it was good. They still stood in the rain with the umbrellas and watched the festival. Despite the rain we had a very good time, because we decided to show something and we showed it rain or sun.'

do? My front room was the room that they make the costumes. I just couldn't get into my front room, there were people everywhere cutting this and cutting that. We had to go along the street with our caps in our hand begging farthings and pennies. Now and then you might get a threepenny bit, but it was a begging thing.

White people took part in it because we got the schools to take part in it, they could put on their own what we call shows. And they could get their own wagon. Most of the people that gave us money were white people anyhow. We were praised after to have brought something like that into St Paul's. We had done something that had never been done before. Because it was really, really dead, dead, dead. St Paul's was a very dead place. Years ago, before, there was gentry lived along City Road, but when I lived there was no gentry in sight. We were just poor people, and Grosvenor Road was a rat-infested place. You could smell it from a mile, it was terrible. But people had to live somewhere, and that was where we could afford.

We have reggae, we have calypso, we have the steel drums, the steel drums came from Bath. Everything we had got to be free because we couldn't afford to pay for it. At the end of we have a dance, called the Festival Dance, which makes a little money, and that's it. This is our way of saying that we have something that we can show you as well, and all of us could enjoy it. We have our music, loud music, and we have our culture. We have dresses and whatever we do was extraordinary, it wasn't something that happened in the streets of England. It was the only one time that we could celebrate and show the locals that we have an idea about celebration. I think they enjoyed it, more than us! Because it's something very new to them, but it's something that we're used to on a yearly basis. It was almost a disaster, because the rain did come down! Everybody have umbrellas up, some people had paper costumes, which were washed away and so forth. But it was good. They still stood in the rain with the umbrella and watched the festival. Despite the rain we had a very good time, because we decided to show something and we showed it rain or sun.

I am very pleased about the things that we done to bring some kind of light to especially St Paul's. We see the changes that have been made in St Paul's. Times change and people change. There are some good changes – the houses that they've built along Grosvenor Road, and other places adjoining to Grosvenor Road, which makes the place look much brighter, more welcoming. St Paul's, the people who live there are very happy, they don't want to leave it. But the sad thing is, we have some renegades that unfortunately come from Jamaica, they call themselves Yardies. And you know, the drugs and the other things that they're doing, is really making it bad for the people who live there. That saddens me. But I've seen a lot of young people do various things, and sometimes I said to myself, I wonder if when I was young I'd have done these things? But if you don't do it now, you won't be able to do it at my age. But do it subtle. Don't hurt anyone. Don't try to hurt anyone.

Roy Hackett lives in St Werburghs, Bristol. He became the first black social worker in Thornbury, and in 1999 he was a recipient of the Royal Maundy at Bristol Cathedral, in recognition of his work with the community.

Mohindra Chowdhry today.

TEN

A PASSAGE TO ENGLAND: MOHINDRA CHOWDHRY

I didn't realise how well off we were, I thought everybody was like that. When that situation was taken away, only then did I realise there are people who are poor. But we became even poorer than them.

I can remember that, as a child, everything looked very big. We did have a very big house, but I wonder whether it would still look as big as I imagine now. I was born in Rawalpindi in 1941, which is Islamabad today, but we lived in Karachi, where my father worked. Where we lived was very comfortable. We could get whatever we wanted to eat. We could go wherever we wanted to go. During the hot summers we went to a hill station where there was a very, very mild climate. We used to have a swimming pool in the house – I remember watching Tarzan films, and imitating him with that dagger on his side and diving in the pool like I was Tarzan! Only thing I didn't have is Cheetah!

There were two ladies who used to clean the house, and two ladies doing the kitchen work with my mother supervising them. My mother used to get up at four o'clock in the morning, do her prayers. After having a shower she would wake up the two ladies who were in charge of the kitchen. They'd make amazing food, which I still remember as some of the best things I ever ate. Then we'd go off to school. At lunchtime, a servant used to come from home with my lunch. And then snacks at four o'clock again, come back, and then the evening meal. I didn't realise how well off we were, I thought everybody was like that. Being too young, I didn't realise. When that situation was taken away, only then did I realise there are people who are poor. But we became even poorer than them.

My father was in the construction business. He was working in Karachi, employing almost 2,000 people. Quite a lot of them were his close relatives and he used to pay them well. But in 1947 it was decided that India was to be divided because the Muslims, Hindus and Sikhs couldn't live together. Overnight things changed. We were told that if we don't leave this part of India which became Pakistan, we shouldn't hope to live very long. One of the drivers who used to work for my Dad told us that our house was going to be targeted, that we were going to be murdered that night – all of us. There was no law and order, you couldn't go to police, you couldn't expect any protection from anybody. But the whole household was ready to defend itself. I remember keeping a knife by my side, to defend myself, although I don't know whether I would have been able to use it. My dad had a dagger, a Kirpan, which by religion Sikhs are supposed to carry with them at all times.

I was so young, it was like a Tarzan adventure story for me. We waited and waited. Any slight movement would give us a jolt. There was nothing to save us if we got attacked. But we were very fortunate that nothing happened and next morning we left the house. Everything we owned, all that money, everything that my parents possessed, even underwear or a handkerchief – there was no time to get it. Whatever we were wearing at that time was what we had. We just walked out and never saw it again. We drove our car to the docks to get a boat to the Indian part, and I remember my Dad handed over the keys to one of the employees he had. He never saw that car again. But for my parents, losing the wealth wasn't that much of a shock. They had two other older sons who were studying in other cities, and for two years they were unable to find out what happened to them. They did turn up safe and sound, but those sons were much more urgent to them than thinking about the wealth they had lost.

We had very, very close relatives living in the north-west frontier, near what is now Islamabad in Pakistan. Sikhs were a minority around there and our relatives were all scattered in small villages. At that time, mobs of hooligans would come and just drag the people out from the houses, set the houses on fire, rape women, take young girls. All those unthinkable things happened. A lot of our relatives decided, 'No, we're not going to go down without a fight,' and they picked up their arms, and fought. Before they fought, they killed their young daughters, because they didn't want them to be dishonoured. Some of them committed suicide and some of them died fighting, and we estimated we must have lost 250 relatives from our family.

The journey to India was very rough, and as soon as we landed in the Indian part we found ourselves living in tents as refugees. We were a family of about ten, and suddenly there was hundreds and hundreds of people like us, living like that. It was a terrible experience. The whole world turned upside down entirely. From a hundred per cent you became zero. You sank to the bottom and I don't think there was anything lower than that. I was used to wearing fresh clothes every day, and I was wearing the same clothes for at least two, three months before things stared to change. I couldn't have bath when I wanted to have bath. When I wanted to have a swim, I couldn't swim.

My mother had come from a rich family, had married a rich man, she'd had a very comfortable life. She really missed having fresh fruit, and I always remember that she would just get a piece of onion and chew on it. We were young kids, so we still managed somehow – but I think she took it very much to heart.

She was very anxious in case something happened to my Dad, who had started working, and started earning money to feed the family, although it was never enough. And she was always telling us – I wish I could die before your Dad does because I don't know how to bring up the family without money. Perhaps her prayers were answered. She used to go the church barefoot, which was what you did if you were very, very devoted. One day she must have walked to church and hit her foot, because she got tetanus, and that evening when I came back from school she was already lying on the bed. She started getting a fever, and the next morning she was dead. We were very close, I've never been closer to anybody else than her. I used to tell her that we'd break out of there, that one day, you don't have to worry; we'll be away from this situation. And I managed it eventually, but she wasn't there to see it.

Eventually we got out of the camp, and went to live in New Delhi. My father worked very hard as a civil engineer. He would leave very early in the morning, about seven o'clock, and he might have to travel miles and miles to get to his site. He'd do his day's work, and come back often nine, ten o'clock in the night, seven days a week. He was earning good money but it was a big family that he had to look after. At the end of the month he used to get his salary. On the way home he would pay off the people who he owed money, you know wherever we used to buy groceries, and things like that. And by the time he came home the majority of the salary was gone. He was insisting that our education must go on, so on top of that he had to school fees for the kids. He did it for years, for years. He was a very healthy man, a very positive man, a very determined man. He never felt sorry for himself, and he worked up to age of seventy-six.

By then, I wanted to get away from India, to a place where I would have some opportunity. Something in me was telling me, no, you are not going to end up here – you are going to do something good. Eventually, I had a chance to come to England. My Dad was against it. He said, 'Stay at home. We will make it here.' And I said, 'No, I want to go, I have to have higher education, and if we are going to compete, I have to have a better quality education.'

And so I came to England, in 1962. I came to Bristol because this was where my Dad's cousins had studied, so it seemed a good place to start. I lived in Stokes Croft, and got a job with John Laing Construction at first. I used to get up six o'clock in the morning and get ready. Eat two eggs and a half-cup of tea, and off to work. The first couple of years were very, very difficult in this country. I'd never been away from my family, and I just couldn't understand people's English here. And when I was trying to speak English to them, they couldn't understand me! So it must have taken me at least six, seven months to understand anything! It was a real big adventure. I was lucky I started working in construction companies and started mixing with common people, because I picked up the slang, and I managed quite well after a while. Every day, after working till half-past five, I used to come back, wash up, get ready, and go to technical college in the evening. Because of the language problem I had to study even harder than every student, but I enjoyed it. I didn't have much social life, and I didn't know many people and I was very serious about my life. But I knew this was only a passing phase.

After a year I started working at Avonmouth docks, painting the cranes. There was one time when I was painting a Goliath crane – some of these cranes are nearly 150 foot high. I remember crawling along it with a paint box and paintbrush in my hand. I don't know what happened – I suddenly slipped from it and fell down straight into the sea! Everything soaking wet, and luckily I landed in the water instead of a ship! There was a boat nearby, and they dragged me out. I had a day off after that, fully paid. But it was a good swim!

I was earning money. I used to send it home to my Dad to look after the other children. Back home the situation was not very good and I wanted them to come out of that poverty that was thrusted on us. I used to write regularly to my father – at least one letter a week, and they used to write also every week one letter. They always encouraged me, always sending me only good news because they knew that I was far away and that any adverse information could affect me.

By now I had been away six years, and I was nearly a qualified civil and structural engineer. My father wrote to me that he wasn't very well, and I knew that if they were informing me it must be very serious. I'd never been able to save money, because I was always sending it back home. But a friend lent me £200 to go home and see him. When he heard I was coming, my father told the doctor who was attending him, 'Look, my son is coming in a day or so – just try

indra as a young man.

to save me from dying for a few days.' And he was still there when I got there. In the end, he pulled out of it and lived almost twenty-five more years after that. I was very glad I went. I had promised him that I will make it, I will get the education, and I'd fulfilled that promise. I wanted personally to convey this message to him – to stand in front of him and tell him. That was very, very important for me, because I couldn't do that with my mother.

While I was there, he said, 'Look, I would like you to have a look at a few girls and see what you think.' And he somehow did this arrangement and I saw this girl – and that was it! I didn't think he was going to move so fast – I didn't realise that. He made arrangements and next day he got me engaged and in another day's time he got me married! I'd never seen her until twenty-four hours

Mohindra and his wife were married in Delhi, India, in 1968. Typical of an Indian marriage, it was arran[g] by Mohindra's father and he met his bride only two days before the wedding. 'The only thing I rememb[er] he showed me a girl and I was married. There was no chance to think about anything – do anything – th[en] was married – that's it!'

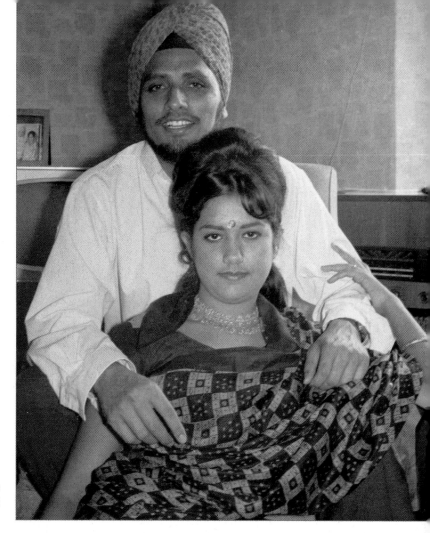

Mohindra and his wife after their arrival in England.

before I was engaged. I didn't know her. But she stayed with me thirty-five years on! Next thing I know, I was coming back to England in less than a week and they sent her over with me to England. She said she's not used to doing any housework, she doesn't know what to do, what not to do, so I said, 'Don't worry, I'll help you.' I had to teach her cooking, I had to teach her how to clean the house, I had to teach her a lot of things. But she was able to catch up really quite quick. I did tell her that in England normally it gets very cold! But she liked Bristol and she did enjoy it, and as a whole she settled well – there was no problem.

We had a daughter, a lovely daughter and then after two and a half years we had a son – a good son. I always wanted to give them a very good education, and I am lucky that I was able to do that. My son is a qualified scientist and now he's an actor. My daughter is a speech therapist and she's married. I really, really enjoy my children. To date I have never ever shouted at them, even when they were young. I've never ever laid a finger on them – they have been my whole,

Here Mohindra is standing outside his first flat in Portland Square, Stokes Croft, Bristol.

whole life. When the children were young and me and my wife we were both very conscious of our accents, and we didn't want our children to pick up that sort of accent from us, so from the very beginning we started taking them to drama school in order to purify their language. To the amazement of both of them, they started winning prizes in acting and Navin, my son, won the best prize in the south-west of England as the best actor. The same year, we put Navin forward for a film with Shirley Maclaine and a superstar from Bombay, and out of thousands and thousands of boys he was selected to play the lead role at age of fifteen and a half. Now, every episode of anything, whatever he has done, on the TV or in the cinema, we watch it, and he has got our full backing and we are very proud of it.

I worked as a civil engineer for fourteen years, and then one fine day I decided that I don't want to be an engineer anymore. I was still young enough to tackle anything, so I started a leather business. By then, the family in India had recovered, and my father was free to do what he liked. He came over here to stay with me. He started enjoying watching the TV. He started playing bridge again, and he joined a bridge club. He started having tea parties. These were things that he missed, and he was able to regain some of those things which he had lost before India was divided. That was very important for us, to show him that we have come to this country, we have worked hard, we have achieved a good standard of life, respect in the community and your sons have managed to do what you expected them to do. I wanted him to see his son, his grandchildren, living in a nice house, driving a good car. He had a good life, with no regrets. He died in 1987 a very happy man, and lived to the ripe age of ninety-two. He was walking until the last day of his life, and he died of old age, that's all.

Religion has been important to me. My religion gave me actual real strength. My faith carried me through.

Mohindra's father.

Without that, I could not have done anything. I learned from my religion, how to respect myself, how to respect other people and be positive and my religion taught me positive thinking. That single factor is the top factor: be positive and work hard. For me, to come to England, and live here and do all those things is fantastic. Some people don't value it, but for me, England has been a very nice journey, and a dream come true.

Mohindra with his wife and children.

Mohindra is sixty-two and lives in Stoke Bishop, Bristol.

Sheila Mitchell Bane today.

ELEVEN

LOVE DOWN UNDER: SHEILA MITCHELL BANE

All the Mr Universes were lined up – Mr New Zealand, Mr Sydney, all of them were lined up. And I looked up at one person and I said to my friend, 'That's the man I want to marry, that one there.'

I always wanted to be a dancer. My feet would bleed from practising and practising at ballet school. My mother and father guessed I would grow out of it, but I practised and practised and I went on lots of trips with my ballet school doing lots of concerts. I still wanted to be a dancer. Then my father was worried. He thought, I don't want my daughter on the stage! I went to a cinema in Staple Hill, the Regal. And I watched Debra Paget in *Princess of the Nile*. I saw her dancing and I said, 'That's what I'm going to do.' Ran home for some more money so that I could see it again, over and over again. And I watched her about ten or fifteen times. And I came home and I said to my mum and dad, 'I want to be a bellydancer.' And mother said to my dad, 'You will have to sort her out! I wash my hands of her!'

I didn't have a boyfriend then, but my girlfriends did. And one was called Killer Brain, and my other girlfriend's, he was called Linky Knot. They all had boyfriends but I didn't because I really wanted to dance and boys got on my nerves at the time. We were the Kingswood Teddy gang. The only place we could go was Kingswood, on the main road, there just wasn't anything else to do. In those days we all carried little vanity cases around. I used to put everything in the vanity case. So when I visited my grandmother, I'd say, 'I'm popping in to see you for an hour,' and by the time she's made me a cup of tea, I've completely changed – my make-up, my hair, the whole lot. And she'd say, 'Are you just visiting me so you can dress up and go up to Kingswood and meet your friends?' I'd say, 'Shh, mum doesn't know.' And off I'd go. You could go up and down this main road, and you could show off to each other. And show your new jacket you bought with the velvet round the top. And show your drop earrings that you borrowed from your mother that she didn't know about. You could bleach your fringe, and wiggle it as you walk along the main road. You'd look at the Teddy boys' suits – drape suits they were, beautiful suits. And their hair, they were always combing their hair. We were just preening ourselves really, and that was all we had to do.

The Teddy boys would congregate sometimes and go off and have their fights. They didn't hurt anyone else, only each other. But my father was very strict. And he could see what was going on by the newspapers and television, and the Teddy boys running riot in the streets of Bristol at the time. And he said, 'I hope you don't get into gangs like this, and go around beating up each other!' 'No father, no.' But the next day, off I'd go to Kingswood, in my gear. Walking up and down, loving every minute. But I still wanted to be a dancer. I

Sheila's parents, pictured here with their children in 1947, decided to emigrate to Australia when Sheila was a teenager. They became one of the Ten Pound Poms encouraged to leave Britain by the cheap £10 fare and the over-the-rainbow dream of a new life in Australia. More than a million Britons went between the end of the war and the early 1970s, helping to swell Australia's population and prosperity.

always seemed to be dancing around and if my father said to me, 'Could you pass me that newspaper over there, Sheila, the *Green 'Un*,' I would do a little pirouette, a little skip and hop, and pass the paper to him. I couldn't keep still. My father was worried about me. But then there was a charity concert at Staple Hill, Page Hall, and I thought, I'm going in for that charity concert. So I did that show and mum came with me to make sure it was all right. She made me the biggest belly dancing costume in Bristol! And I went into the concert and I won it. I was so proud of myself and I said to my mum and dad, 'I'm definitely going to be a dancer now.'

One day, I could hear mother and father discussing Australia in the front room while I was in the back room. And I could hear them saying, 'Well, if we go to Australia, we may never see our parents again.' And my dad said, 'Well, we'll have to try and make an effort. There's nothing here for us, we're just carrying on, things aren't good, we're not getting on very well. Let's go and make a fresh life, let's go to Australia. I've got to let them know by next week. And I know they'll look after us, I know there's a job because they've offered me a job in Australia. I know it'll be hard for Sheila and Bob, I know everything will work out OK.' Eventually, dad did come out to tell me we were definitely going. And I said to my dad, 'What about my friends? You're taking me away from my friends. How could you do that?' And he looked at me as if to say, 'Yes, I know your friends, those Teddy boys at Kingswood!' So we decided to go. I didn't want to go, but I did it for my father. So we had to pack. It was only one crate we were allowed to take at the time, like all the other immigrants to Australia, one crate we were allowed. Mum packed all her personal belongings into this crate. And she decided to buy some bone china. A dinner set of bone china. She said, 'I'll take something English with me.' A whole dinner set of bone china, very proud of that. So they packed that into the crate and then off we went to Dover.

We had to leave my mum and dad's parents behind, which was a big wrench for them. 'Cause in those days, in the 1950s, there was no coming back. Not that easy, anyway. And of course, you don't know if you're going to see your parents again. So we went to Dover, and we were boarding the ship, very, very nervous. This old troop ship, hundreds of immigrants, all very nervous, and families saying goodbye. And we were watching them loading the crates on as we were on the ship, and I saw my dad say to my mother, 'Ooh look, our crate's next! Here she goes!' And it crashed right into the side of the ship. The crate opened up and all mum's china came out. All fell into the sea. My mum turned to my father and cried her eyes out. She said, 'See! We shouldn't be going, should we? We shouldn't be going.' And he said, 'We're on our way now,' and then we set on our way. And I think they played the *Dambusters' March* as we sailed out.

Some landed in Melbourne and some landed in Sydney. And as they got off the ship, they then had to go to their various destinations. Lots of them were going to camps. Luckily we had some friends in the outback. Our friends had emigrated about ten years previously. We went to them and they said if you wish, we have quite a bit of land, you can build a temporary dwelling in the field over there. And they set about building this shed, and it was a shed because there was no lining or anything like that. And they build this shed. My mother's face dropping and dropping thinking, 'What have we done? Why have we come out here?' And then of course, there was no fridges, didn't have fridges in those days. We had ice blocks that were dropped off by transport. We had a tank at the back of the shed. And they would deliver water to us every week. And we also had a toilet down at the back of the garden, which we used to have a big spray handy. We had to spray all round the doorway and the toilet because of the funnel webs. And the redbacks.

I had a tiny little room – it was just a separation in-between. And my brother slept on the settee. And mum and dad had a little partitioned-off room. And I can remember lying in bed watching white lizards running all over the walls and the ceiling. I didn't mind that. I could hear the mosquitoes buzzing round my head. And one day I was in the yard. I was walking to the toilet and I saw an iguana. It was like a dragon to me then, I didn't know how to react. So I had to wait for the iguana to go away before I could go to the toilet. And the biggest spiders they had in Australia were the rain spiders. They were big as my hand. They were the only ones that won't kill you. But of course, I was scared to death of these big rain spiders. They would just sit on the wall and wouldn't move, so you wouldn't know that they were there. You see a leg move, and you stand there stunned, because you can't believe how big these spiders are, and yet they wouldn't hurt you. The Australians wouldn't take any notice, they'd just put them out or push them aside. But we English hadn't seen anything like that before, so we were really, really scared. We wanted to come home. And why did we come out to Australia? We blamed my father for bringing us out there. And I missed my Teddy boys.

I was so homesick, I was crying every night, I would cry and cry. But I really liked the Australians, and I soon began to like Australia itself. I eventually found a job that I really wanted to do. I worked in the American Health Studio in Sydney. I was a keep-fit instructor, and I loved my job. And I thought if I

Sheila in Menai, Australia, when she was sixteen.

Sheila first saw her future husband Peter (far left) when he was doing a Mr Universe show in Sydney in 1960. She took one look at him and said, 'That's the man I want to marry, that one there.'

keep fit and do this job, I can also dance on evenings. One night my colleagues decided we would go to the Latin Quarter, a nightclub, because there was the Mr Universe show there. So we all decided to go to this club, and it was brilliant. And all the Mr Universes were lined up – Mr New Zealand, Mr Sydney, Mr Universe, all of them were lined up. And I looked up at one person and I said to my friend, 'That's the man I want to marry, that one there.' And my friend turned to me and said, 'That's strange, he's the only English one in the show.' And then I forgot all about it.

A few days later he turned up at the club because he wanted to do some weight-training. So my friend introduced him to me. We went out in the day, and we got on very well. I fell in love instantly with him, but I can't put my finger on why. I just fell in love with him, and wanted to be with him. Even though he was Mr Universe and all the muscles went with it, I didn't take much

...la and Peter decided to start an act together, where she would dance and he would flex his Mr Universe ...sique. This is one of their first publicity shots, taken on a beach in Sydney.

notice of that because I was already working in the health studio, so you were seeing those shapes and bodies every day. I got used to that. I don't know if I was attracted to him because he was English as well, but we seemed to gel together, as if I'd known him for years. I just felt I wanted to be with him forever and we just seemed to have the same interests, and things like that. He was also in this show for about a month. He made friends with the choreographer, and she was about to retire. And she said, seeing as your friend is also a dancer, could I form an act for you? Perhaps you could tour the clubs in Sydney, and work in all the legions, all the RSL [Returned and Services League] clubs, then you could make lots of money and enjoy your work. So we decided to do that weekends, and we practised for it, and we became a very good act.

At the time my mother and father were very unhappy. My father was very, very homesick. And he missed his local pub, and he missed the football and he missed meeting his friends in the village. He said, 'I must go home.' And I said to my parents, 'Well, I've met someone now, I'd like you to meet him.' So they met Peter, and they said, 'Well, we're going back in a few months' time, you will be coming back with us.' And I said, I don't think so. And they said, 'You must.' I said, 'I don't think so.' I said, 'I'm going to marry him.' So I married Peter, and they gave us a lovely wedding in Australia. Although my father didn't want me to marry Peter, I was twenty-one and he did see that I was very much in love with Peter and he was the only one I wanted to marry. So, in the end he had to give in, he'd rather he left me married than leave me just wandering around Sydney. They liked Peter very much, but they thought he was the sort of person that might travel and wander around the world, and not stay at home and be a husband. But little did they know, I didn't want to stay at home at the time anyway, so we would have been perfect together. And also we were practising for this act we were doing together, and we were approached by an agent, who asked us if we would go into the circus and travel round Australia for a year. And so we decided to say yes, so we could see Australia.

It was a very hard time we had in the circus, we were travelling days and days on dusty roads, and then we'd finish up in huge fields. We all had jobs to do, and we'd have tent hands. There were other acts that were with us, caravan convoys. And we'd be very tired when we got to these places, but we loved every minute. And I'd have to help with the tenting, and placing all the seats in the tent. And Peter would bang in all the pegs, 'cause he could do that in about two hits. So we loved all those little jobs. So we travelled for a whole year and then finished up back in Sydney again. So we did this act, and we thought we're doing very well with this. We worked in Sydney, all the clubs, and we decided

The Fabulous
Mr. UNIVERSE
and
Miss VENUS

e Fabulous Mr Universe and Miss Venus
yed all over Australia and the Far East,
omising 'Mr Universe with his fabulous
scle control, moves every muscle in his
dy to music. This has to be seen to be
ieved. Miss Venus performs various
ces including Bedroom Dream and
waiian. Finishing with their spectacular
agio Act, these brilliant performers have
ned a worldwide reputation.'

Left: Sheila had always wanted to dance, and for a while her dreams came true and her and Peter's act gradually became more successful.

Right and opposite: Sheila and Peter – seen here in Hong Kong in 1964 – spent most of the early 1960s touring the Far East, including Thailand, Laos, Cambodia, Singapore and Taiwan, and entertaining American troops in Saigon during the Vietnam War. 'We saw a lot of things in the Far East we didn't like – the sadness and poverty. Entertaining the troops in Saigon upset me very badly because of the violence we saw there.'

we'd like to travel to the Far East. And Hong Kong. They would love Mr Universe. So we set about doing a tour for about a year to two years. And we travelled about the Far East, setting off to Japan first, three shows a night, twenty-one shows a week. And we moved on from Hong Kong to Taiwan, Singapore, Laos, Cambodia, Saigon – we entertained the troops in Saigon. Our act was that I would dance first of all, and then I would fall asleep on a couch. And I would dream of my dream man, and the lights would go out, and a spotlight would come on, on to the stage, on to a plinth. And there was Mr Universe. And Mr Universe would pose to Swan Lake. And a small spotlight came on to my face, and I would dream of him. He would do muscle control to *Tea for Two* cha-cha. And the audience would laugh. And the more they laughed, the more he did all the muscle control. And then the lights would go out, the two spots would go on both of us, and then we would do Samson and Delilah. An adagio act, acrobatic adagio act. So it was like a dream came true. I think lots of people looked on our act as a romantic, Romeo and Juliet type thing.

Things started to go downhill after about three years. We saw a lot of things in the Far East we didn't like – the sadness and poverty. The children's poverty I couldn't stand any longer. Entertaining the troops in Saigon upset me very badly. I lost weight, went down to seven and a half stone. When we were entertaining the troops in Saigon, I became very ill. And I was sick most of the time, so I would lie down in between the shows, and then go back and do the shows for the GIs, and then go back and lie down again. I realised it wasn't the food I was eating. And my costumes wouldn't fit any more and I had a job to get my costumes round my body. My body was swollen. The doctor said I was three months pregnant, and that if I didn't stop doing acrobatics now I would lose the baby. I went back to tell Peter my husband and said, I'm afraid we're gonna have to finish. We were both in shock actually because we didn't think we would have children yet and of course we still had two contracts to fulfil in the Far East. I said, 'I am not going to lose this baby.' So we decided then that we'd leave the contracts behind and go back to Sydney, and we'd have Tracy in Sydney, where I knew the hospital and I knew the place. I wanted to go back.

When we came back from the Far East and I was having Tracy, Peter then realised he was just Peter. He was not the celebrity he was in the Far East, where we'd have hired cars, limousines, they'd bow to us as we entered the club. When we went back to Sydney and had Tracy, we reached reality then. I did do showbusiness with him for a little while in Sydney. But we couldn't do that for ever, and there is a lifespan that you can do in showbusiness. And I felt that it came to the end. But he couldn't see that. We didn't have a house, we had hotel

Right: When this photograph was taken in Singapore, Sheila didn't realise that she was two months pregnant with her daughter.

Left: By 1965, Sheila was beginning to tire of touring and was losing weight. This was one of their last shows in Hong Kong.

rooms, we lived in suitcases. And there was no way that he was going out to find a job that would support us at the time. He was just lost really. So Peter started to drink and he was drinking very heavily. He couldn't control his drinking, so when he was drinking he wasn't eating, so when he wasn't eating he wasn't training. Of course, we couldn't do the shows as we wanted to, to the standard we wanted. Because he was losing weight then and he was drinking heavily. I was worried if we did acrobatics he'd drop me and I'd break my neck.

Sadly the drink got the better of him. There was no facilities in Sydney in those days in the 1950s and 60s. There was nowhere you could go when you needed help, there was only the Catholic Church or the Salvation Army. He changed character, and he wasn't the man I married. He wasn't Mr Universe, he wasn't Peter my husband; it was a change in character. He was a changed man, and he was a strong man, and I thought if I stayed with him any longer he would become very, very aggressive. He may never know what he's done. I didn't want to go, but there was no alternative in those days. I had nowhere else to go and there was no help. It just got worse and worse. He could see he was losing me. And he had nowhere to go, so he just drank more and drank more. He was a celebrity but he'd fallen, and he didn't know how to pick himself up. I was quite willing to have done a cleaning job, but he didn't want me to do that, because he was a celebrity. And he found it hard, he just found it hard, that he wasn't Mr Universe anymore.

My mum and dad were in Melbourne then 'cause dad was working for BOAC for a six-month contract. And they came up to visit us in Sydney, saw the baby, Peter and me. The baby was very happy and healthy, but we weren't happy and we weren't healthy. My mum could see there was a big problem there, and she could see Peter was struggling. My parents tried very, very hard to keep us together and bring us together, but in the end we had to consider the future of my daughter. My parents had already gone back to England and come back again. So they said, 'We've tried everything for you to be together now, there doesn't seem to be any hope. You seem to be falling apart.' I had to make a decision then, about my husband and my baby. I decided to come back to England with my parents, and bring my baby with me. And leave my husband in Sydney for him to make a fresh life. So it was very, very sad. When it came time for me to get on the ship, Peter was there. So I went over to say goodbye to him, and he said, 'Why are you taking my baby away from me?' I said, 'The only choice I've at the moment is to go back to England with my parents and take Tracy. For our sakes, Peter, and for Tracy's sake, I'm going back to England. I have to go.' And I left him, stood by himself as we got on the ship. And I had

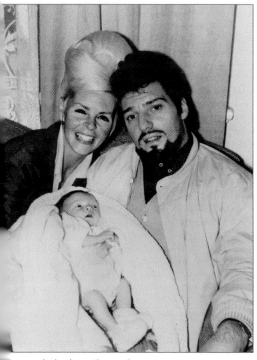

ter and Sheila with newborn Tracy.

Tracy meeting Peter and his mother.

to turn away. I did the right thing, although I wish it had worked out for us really. But fate's not like that, is it?

So I went back to England. I settled into home, Tracy went to school, I found a job and I settled into my village life again. Peter tried to contact me a couple of times to try to get me to go back to Australia. But of course, I didn't want to go back to Australia again. In the end, I think he got worse and worse and he had cirrhosis of the liver. So I know I did the right thing by coming back to England. But he wanted to meet Tracy. So we arranged that Tracy would meet her dad for the first time, and stay with his mother for a week. I never met Peter, I didn't want to. I just turned my back, I just wanted my memories. He went back to Australia and died within a few weeks. So we just had a feeling that he knew he wasn't a well man, and just wanted to see Tracy. So I'm glad he did it. And I feel now, I've gone all the way round the world and I've come back to where I started. But I've got no regrets, and I'm very happy and contented now.

Sheila Mitchell Bane still lives in Bristol near her daughter.

TWELVE

MAKING HISTORY

This final chapter suggests ways of recording your own personal or family history of the British Empire and Commonwealth. Today, a renewed fascination with history, along with a fashion for oral history and genealogy, means that the lives and experiences of older relatives and friends are newly valued. Many people want to preserve this history, these pictures and tales of the past, for grandchildren and future generations.

This section places the emphasis on video history, rather than the traditional audio-taped oral history, because film offers a third dimension that a taped voice cannot: the expressive nature of the face, with a language and emotional power all of its own. Because of this, video recordings are potentially the most powerful form of oral history.

WHAT IS ORAL HISTORY?

Oral history is spoken history, recorded and preserved for the future. Many of the ancient historical sources we rely on today came from oral testimony that was later written down, testimony that was passed on from generation to generation purely by word of mouth – through stories, folklore, myths and songs. It involves preserving someone's life story on tape, along with his or her local dialect or way of speaking, and important details of their family life, education, traditions and beliefs, work and achievements. It differs from conventional history in that people are able to talk about their feelings and emotions, and it gives 'ordinary' people – rather than world leaders, politicians or celebrities – the chance to talk about how they felt about their everyday life, or how they faced momentous periods of history like the Partition of India. The great strength of oral history is its subjectivity and its personal depth. By delving into an individual's life it offers unique insights and new perspectives. It can also give value and meaning to forgotten lives.

WHAT AND WHOM TO FILM

The beauty of oral history is that it includes everyone, so that those whose histories are often hidden, particularly ethnic minorities and marginalized groups, get a chance to speak. Generally speaking, recording the oral histories of those who lived in the empire and commonwealth, or those who travelled to Britain from there, is straightforward. But you should keep the following in mind when recording any kind of history:

- Some people have religious or cultural traditions that you need to be aware of, so try to be culturally sensitive.

- Remember that those who lived through an event like the Second World War, the independence of a country or racial discrimination may have experienced traumatic events. They may have suffered personal loss or heartbreak. Always treat people's memories gently and with respect.

Many people want to film their family history. For instance, your grandfather may have grown up in colonial Kenya or come to England from Jamaica in the 1950s, or your mother may have spent her childhood in British Cyprus or fled Idi Amin's brutal rule in Uganda. It is often interesting to film several generations of a family to chart the changes in society over the years, as well as their differing experiences. The children of Jamaican immigrants from the 1950s will often have very different views and opinions about Britain and its imperial history from their grandchildren.

You could also think of a theme or topic related to the British Empire and Commonwealth and then interview a number of related or unrelated people about it. For instance, you could focus on your street or your area, memories of a childhood abroad, a religion, Caribbean immigration in the 1950s, the Second World War, a first love, a political event or memories of emigrating. It's important to get a grip of your subject before you start, and your local library or record office should have plenty of books, maps and old newspapers to get you started.

If you're focusing on a theme, there are lots of ways of finding contributors or people to interview. Ask friends and relatives, neighbours and work colleagues. Older people's clubs, local history groups and voluntary organisations may be able to help. One of the most effective ways of finding people to interview is to place a letter in the letters page of your local newspaper asking for contributors

Opposite, above: Norman Jones's army colleagues in the Malayan jungle in 1953.
Opposite, below: Hazel Hooper's school chums in Madras in India, around 1925, at the height of British power in India.

11 PLATOON
JAN. 1953

INESON   LT. SHAPLAND   FRANKLIN   JONES   SMITH. 17

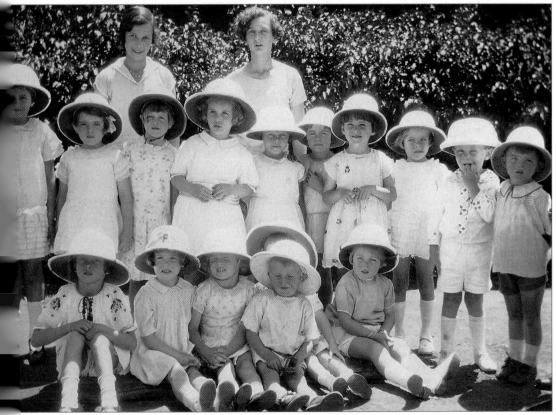

Edward Prince of Wales (right) on safari in Tanzania in 1927.

Hazel Hooper and her twin sister on the long voyage from India back to England in 1926, on their way boarding school.

or to make an appeal on local radio. When you're choosing who to film, try to get a good cross section, including men and women, a mixture of social class backgrounds and ethnic minorities. Although it is important to film people who are articulate and can speak fairly clearly, don't always go for the chatty ones. Those who are naturally shy have a history too.

RECORDING THE PAST

It is quite understandable that a lack of expertise and a fear of technology put many people off filming oral history. But this need not be the case, since so many people have basic video cameras these days, and it really is just one step up from making your own holiday video. The advent of cheap, miniature and easy-to-use digital video (DV) cameras in recent years has revolutionised the audio-visual market.

It is now possible to buy a good quality DV camera for around £500 – Sony and Canon both do decent models around this price (try www.sony.co.uk or www.canondv.com). More professional cameras – the Sony DSR PD150 or DCR VX2000 – cost around £2,500, but can be hired from local suppliers. In addition, the other vital pieces of kit are a tripod and good microphones – good sound is very important for a professional-looking film. For a straightforward one-to-one interview you'll need tie-clip microphones that plug into the camera, one for you and one for your contributor, or you can use a uni-directional hand-held microphone.

There is an increasing number of training courses available that teach all aspects of film-making using DV cameras, many of which are aimed at non-professionals. Online there are also some excellent resources, particularly the BBC's training pages, which give a free guide to the more advanced DV cameras (www.bbctraining.co.uk/television.asp).

Of course this could all end up being very expensive, and there are plenty of local history societies, schools and universities that have cameras and microphones they may be willing to lend or hire out. We've written this as a guide to video history, but you could just as well record people's memories on audiotape.

Again, you will probably be able to find a group that will lend or hire a tape recorder, but otherwise the better mini-tape recorders on the market are the Sony Professional Walkman or the high quality Marantz 230 or 430 tape recorder. For good sound quality, it is better not to rely on the recorder's own built-in microphone, so, if you can, plug a separate microphone into the recorder instead.

Making sure that you are prepared before an interview and that you have all the right equipment is vital if everything is to go smoothly.

BEFORE THE INTERVIEW

You've chosen your contributors, and you've got to know about their life stories. It will now help you if you prepare a list of questions for the interview. Unless you're doing something very specific, it's good to try to cover the following:

- Name, date and place of birth
- Parents' occupations
- Family background, grandparents
- Childhood at home – housework, chores, mealtimes, discipline
- Leisure – street games, sports, clubs, weekends, holidays, festivals
- Schooling – teachers, friends, subjects, discipline
- Early relationships
- Working life – first job, typical working day, promotion, unions, etc.
- Family life – children, homes, money, neighbours
- Marriage/divorce
- Social life
- Politics and religion
- Hopes for the future

SETTING UP THE INTERVIEW

- It is generally better to film people in their own homes, as long as they are comfortable with this and you feel safe doing so. Make the day and time you're coming clear, and confirm it the day before. Also, make sure that you've set aside enough time – it takes a while to prepare your equipment and set up the room, and the interview itself may be at least an hour long.

- Check you've got all the right kit before you go to the interview – have you got the right power supply or batteries for your camera and microphones? Have you got your DV tapes or audiocassettes? Do you have all the paperwork you're going to need, and your list of questions?

- TV film interviews often involve at least three or four people. If you're filming, you'll find it easier to take another person with you to run the camera. That way you'll have more time to spend relaxing your contributor and concentrating on the interview.

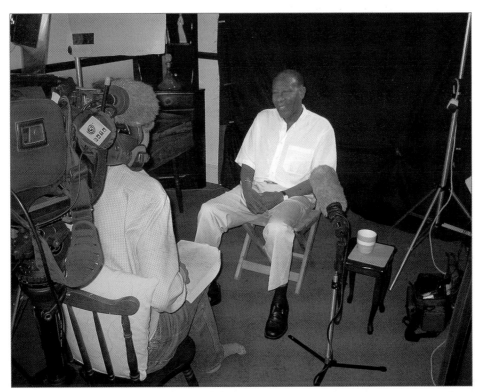

Relaxed, smiling contributors give much better interviews, so try to create an atmosphere that's calm and peaceful.

- Find a good, light location for the interview – cosy sofa and pictures, or a plain wall or backdrop (don't use professional lights unless you've been trained to do so – they can be dangerous and difficult to use).
- Make sure the room is quiet, away from busy roads and loud noise. Ask if you can switch off radios or televisions, and remember to look out for crackling fires, buzzing fridges and ticking clocks, as well as nervous or over-excited pets.
- Always film interviews using a tripod – wobbly pictures look most unprofessional.
- Most interviews are filmed with the interviewee looking at the interviewer off camera. So sit close to the interviewee, but make sure you can't be seen. The other way to do it is to have the interviewee talking straight into the camera, but this is much more difficult to do because his or her instinct will always be to look towards you.
- Take time to frame the interview well – a simple head and upper body shot works well, or just head and shoulders. You can also film people to one side of the screen, but make sure that they're not going to move out of shot.
- Check your sound levels – if you're using tie-clip microphones make sure they're attached to clothing at the top of the chest, and are not brushing against clothes or jewellery, or put your hand-held microphone about nine to twelve inches away from your contributor's mouth.
- Before you start, switch on the tape and state who you're interviewing and where they live, just in case you lose your paperwork.

The Interview

Unless the person you are interviewing has told his or her story many times before, he or she will almost certainly be nervous, so the most important thing is to be polite and patient. Make sure you have a conversation before an interview to put people at their ease – the word interview terrifies a lot of people, so explain that you're just going to have a friendly chat. Explain that they need to look at you, and not at the camera, during the interview. And if you're going to edit the interview later, you may want to cut your questions out. If you do, ask people to answer in a full sentence, with some of the question in the answer. So, the answer to the question 'Where were you born?' would be, 'I was born in Jamaica,' rather than just 'Jamaica'.

You're now ready to start the interview. You're probably nervous too, but try to keep the following things in mind:

ake sure you take time to get to know your contributors well before the interview, and that you put their
nd at rest about any fears they might have about talking about the past.

- It is up to you to guide the interview and to ensure your interviewee is
  relaxed. Keep nodding and smiling, offer lots of encouragement between
  questions, and don't hurry. Listen carefully and maintain good eye contact.
- Start at the beginning, asking your interviewees their full name and when
  and where they were born. Use your list of questions, but don't be tied to
  them. The interview will lead you to questions you won't have thought of,
  and possibly information you weren't expecting.
- Concentrate on the actual details and incidents of a life, not second-hand
  hearsay. Eyewitness testimony is what you're looking for.
- Clarify words or anything you're not sure of at the time, rather than later.
- Try not to interrupt, and do give your interviewee the time to answer.
  Don't contradict and don't get into an argument.
- If your interviewee is older, be aware that they may get tired, or a need a
  break or a glass of water. It's often worth splitting the interview into
  several sessions if people have a lot to tell you.

After the interview, don't rush away. Take time to look at old photographs or documents, and to offer reassurance about the interview. Make sure you have your interviewee's address and phone number, and confirm any future appointments, especially if your interview is going to be in several parts.

If the people you are interviewing are not members of the family, the other thing you need to do is to get them to fill in a copyright form. Copyright is a complicated issue. Essentially, they own the copyright on their spoken words, but you own the copyright to the actual recording you've made. Oral history is classed as a form of intellectual property, so you have to have permission from the contributor to use it in any form. It is also important to know that any people mentioned in the interview are 'data subjects', and have copyright rights too. So be very careful about releasing material into the public domain that is very personal, or may upset living persons.

You can download a basic form from the East Midlands Oral History Association's excellent website at www.le.ac.uk/emoha/training/no4.pdf. Explain to interviewees that you're not allowed to use their interview unless they sign the form, and assure them that you will only use it for the purposes you've agreed. Make sure they sign the form on the day, as going back later can complicate matters.

FINISHING YOUR FILM

For many people, having a full, professional-looking interview on film is enough, particularly if you're interviewing family members for posterity. But if you want to make a finished film, you can do so by editing down the interview and intercutting relevant pictures. This is quite a complicated process, and it may not be worth doing if you don't have a lot of time to invest in it. First, you need to make a list of what was said in the interview, with timings if your camera has these. It may help you to transcribe the interview word for word into a transcript, but beware that this is extremely time consuming, and that it can take about six hours to transcribe an hour of tape.

The idea then is to compile a script, which tells the life story of your contributor or contributors, composed of the most interesting bits of interview intercut with your pictures. These could be old photos that you've filmed with your DV camera, old home movies or extra shots of your area, house or contributors that you've filmed yourself. You might also find material from your local newspaper or library. Use your script as a guide when editing. Professional editing is a very expensive process, costing thousands of pounds, but the new

PC-based editing packages such as Premier and Final Cut Pro mean that you can edit your DV film inexpensively and comparatively easily on your home PC. Some of these editing packages can be bought for less than £100.

WHAT NEXT?

Recently, groups in the south-west have begun experimenting with video history, with some interesting results. A shining example is the Elders' Forum at the Malcolm X Centre on City Road in St Paul's. Its members are mainly Afro-Caribbean men and women, and it was their idea to share their experiences with the younger generation in the area by making a video. The aim was to get the elders trained in film-making, so that they could record their memories, songs and photographs, and make a finished film that could easily be shown anywhere. But what did they hope to get out of the project? Jessica Titus-Glover, one of the elders, says, 'My children were born here, so they don't know

St Paul's in 1963.

The Elders' Forum at the Malcolm X Centre recently completed a video history including songs and recipe along with their own stories and memories.

about my roots, but I teach it to them. I don't want them not to know, it's a legacy that should be handed down from one generation to the next.'

Having got funding, they decided to go ahead. The group was very big – about thirty enthusiastic people. As they learnt to film each other, they were creating the interviews for the final film, as well as a valuable and fascinating archive. Eventually a core small group took charge of the structure and editing of the piece – looking at archive material, using interview transcripts and linking up sequences – as well as some of the more technical side of the editing process. Although progress was quite slow, and working with such a big group was challenging, team leader Cluna Donnelly thinks the project has been very successful. 'The feedback from the group has been really good. In the end, the experience of making the film was more about valuing themselves, their stories and passing on a legacy than purely about the "course" or the technical learning experience.' Team member Esther Phillips says, 'We made way for the young people today. They would never put up with what we had to in those days.' Making the video has meant that the memories and experiences of those pioneers from Jamaica and Barbados will not be forgotten, and that their history is valued.

So, what can you do with your finished film? Your project may well have been done for your own personal pleasure, or with a group like the Elders' Forum, or to keep in the family as a record for future generations, but there are plenty of ways of displaying your work to the public if you want to. If you've made a complete film, you could try showing it at a local museum or community centre. You could also deposit copies of your tapes and transcripts with your local library or history society to add to their archive – or with a bigger organisation like the British Empire and Commonwealth Museum. Finally, oral history is increasingly being put on the web. There is a growing number of excellent sites dedicated to ethnic minority oral history, detailed in the resources section at the end of this book. If you think you'd like to have a go at creating your own website, have a look at the guidelines at www.le.ac.uk/emoha/training/no11.pdf. Good luck!

Schoolchildren in St Paul's.

THE BRITISH EMPIRE AND COMMONWEALTH MUSEUM

The British Empire and Commonwealth Museum has spent ten years collecting oral history interviews reflecting every aspect of the empire. The collection covers a vast range of views, opinions, anecdotes and experience from people who lived and worked in the former empire and commonwealth. There are stories about administrators, nurses, foresters, agriculturalists, geologists, explorers and colonial wives, among others. There are stories about living in isolated and remote areas of the world, with topics ranging from tiger hunts and parties to daily life and injustice. The interviews recall a time that is almost gone – they make fascinating listening.

The main part of the collection consists mainly of British citizens who lived and worked in the countries that made up the former empire and commonwealth. The museum also holds special collections that include: commonwealth soldiers, the South African collection, exploration, original interviews and transcripts from radio and TV, Indian nationalists and Mau Mau freedom fighters. There is also a growing collection of the oral history of the many indigenous peoples who lived under British rule. The catalogue of the archive, *Voices and Echoes*, is available from the British Empire and Commonwealth Museum in Bristol.

Opposite page: Testimony Films' video display at the British Empire and Commonwealth Museum is set out like a tiny cinema and shows a rich variety of people telling their stories, whether they lived in British India or worked as missionaries in Kenya or came to Britain to live and work – like Mohindra Chowdhry from Bristol.

Notes

CHAPTER 1

1 Recent studies of the south-west's history and interaction with the empire include Madge
   Dresser's *Slavery Obscured: A Social History of Slavery in an English Provincial Port* (2001),
   and a forthcoming history of the ethnic minority communities in the area, produced by
   the Kuumba Project in Bristol.
2 See David Richardson, *The Bristol Slave Traders: A Collective Portrait* (1985).
3 See Peter Fryer, *Staying Power: The History of Black People in Britain* (1984).
4 See C.M. McInnes, *Bristol: Gateway of Empire* (1978).

Further Reading

EMPIRE AND COMMONWEALTH HISTORY

Ashcroft, Bill (ed.), *The Empire Writes Back: Theory and Practice in Post-Colonial Literatures (New Accents)*, Routledge, 2002

Bean, Philip and Melville, Joy, *Lost Children of the Empire*, Unwin Hyman Ltd, 1989

Cannock, Marion, *The Precious McKenzie Story*, Pelham Books, 1975

Ferguson, Niall, *Empire*, Penguin Press, 2003

Fryer, Peter, *Staying Power: The History of Black People in Britain*, Pluto Press, 1984

Humphreys, Margaret, *Empty Cradles: One Woman's Fight to Uncover Britain's Most Shameful Secret*, Doubleday, 1994

Huxley, Elspeth, *The Flame Trees of Thika: Memories of an African Childhood*, Chatto & Windus, 1987

James, Laurence, *The Rise and Fall of the British Empire*, Little, Brown and Company, 1998

Killingray, David, *Africans in Britain*, Frank Cass and Company Ltd, 1994

Phillips, Trevor and Phillips, Mike, *Windrush: The Irresistible Rise of Multi-Racial Britain*, HarperCollins Publishers, 1998

Visram, Rozina, *Asian in Britain: 400 Years of History*, Pluto Press, 2002

Wambu, Onyekachi (ed.), *Empire Windrush: Fifty Years of Writing about Black Britain*, Phoenix, 1999

SOUTH-WEST HISTORY

Dresser, Madge, *Black and White on the Buses: The 1963 Colour Bar Dispute in Bristol*, Bristol Broadsides (Co-op) Ltd, 1986

Jones, Donald, *Bristol Past*, Phillimore and Company Ltd, 2000

Kuumba, *Origins: Personal Stories of Crossing the Sea to Settle in Britain*, Origins/Halsgrove Books, 1998

Lindegaard, D., *Black Bristolians in the Eighteenth and Nineteenth Centuries*, Bristol Reference Library, n.d.

McInnes, Charles Malcolm, *Bristol: Gateway of Empire*, David and Charles Ltd, 1968

Marshall, Peter, *Bristol and the Abolition of Slavery*, Bristol Branch of the Historical Association, 1975

Pryce, Ken, *Endless Pressure: A Study of West Indian Lifestyles in Bristol*, Bristol Classical Press, 1986

Richardson, David, *The Bristol Slave Traders: A Collective Portrait*, Alan Sutton Publishing Ltd, 1985

ORAL HISTORY

British Empire and Commonwealth Museum, *Voices and Echoes: British Empire and Commonwealth Museum Oral History Holdings*, British Empire and Commonwealth Museum, 1999

Frances, Vivienne, *With Hope in their Eyes*, X Press, 1998

Perks, Robert and Thomson, Alistair (eds), *The Oral History Reader*, Routledge, 1998

Terkel, Studs, *My American Century*, W. W. Norton & Co. Inc., 1997

LOCAL ORAL HISTORY

African-Caribbean Community in Gloucestershire, The, *Our Untold Stories: The African Caribbean Community in Gloucestershire*, Gloucestershire County Libraries, 2001

Asian Community in Gloucestershire, The, *Our Untold Stories: The Asian Community in Gloucestershire*, Gloucestershire County Libraries, 2003

Chinese Community in Gloucestershire, The, *Our Untold Stories: The Chinese Community in Gloucestershire*, Gloucestershire County Libraries, 2001

Collins, Sharon and Begum, Helen, *Hidden Voices: A Study of Wiltshire's Minority Ethnic Residents*, Wiltshire County Council REC, 2002

Fairfield House Senior Citizens Project, *A Sweet and Sour Journey: Reminiscing with the Senior Citizens Project at Fairfield House*, Bath & North East Somerset Council's Linear Way Industries, 1998

Fairfield House Senior Citizens Project, *Spice Routes to Bath: Recipes from Fairfield House Senior Citizens Project*, Bath & North East Somerset Council's Linear Way Industries, 2001

Green, Carlton, *High Hopes and Great Expectations: From Jamaica to England . . . One Man's View*, Carlton Green, 2000

Johnson, Gail, *A Long Five Years: Caribbean Elders in Gloucester*, 'A Long Five Years' Project, 1995

Muktodhara – Bengalis in Bristol, St Werberghs Community Centre

Oral History Resources

SOUTH-WEST

British Empire and Commonwealth Museum
Address: British Empire and Commonwealth Museum, Clock Tower Yard, Temple Meads, Bristol, BS1 6QH, UK
Tel: 0117 925 4980
Fax: 0117 925 4983
Email: admin@empiremuseum.co.uk
Website: http://www.empiremuseum.co.uk/
A publicly accessible history of the British Empire that also examines its continuing impact on Britain and the rest of the world. The galleries use a mix of authentic objects, costume, film, photographs and sound recordings, many never seen before in public. The museum holds an extensive oral history collection.

Kuumba Arts Project
Address: 20–23 Hepburn Road, St Paul's, Bristol BS2 8UD, UK
Tel: 0117 942 1870
Kuumba is an important centre for black art and culture, showing theatre and film and running writers' workshops and an excellent library, as well as occasional black elders' oral history workshops.

Malcolm X Centre
Address: 141 City Road, St Paul's, Bristol BS2 8YH, UK
Tel: 0117 955 4497
This well-known community centre in St Paul's caters for the black community in the area, and hosts the Elders' Forum mentioned in the final chapter.

Bristol Central Library
Address: College Green, Bristol BS1 5TL, UK
Tel: 0117 903 7200
Email: bristol_library_service@bristol-city.gov.uk
Website: www.bristol-city.gov.uk
The library has an excellent local history section in its reference library, as well as a wide range of books on the British Empire and Commonwealth and its history.

Bristol Public Record Office Picture Library
Address: 'B' Bond Warehouse, Smeaton Road, Bristol BS1 6XN, UK
Tel: 0117 922 4224
Website: http://www.bristol-city.gov.uk/rec–office/record-office.html
Holds a wide range of documents, pictures, photographs and artefacts relating to the history of Bristol and the surrounding area, with extremely helpful staff. Many of its holdings are catalogued and available online.

NATIONAL GROUPS

Oral History Society
Address: The Secretary, Oral History Society, c/o Department of History, University of Essex, Colchester CO4 3SQ, UK
Tel: 0207 412 7405
Email: rob.perks@bl.uk
Website: www.oralhistory.org.uk
The Oral History Society is a national and international organization dedicated to the collection and preservation of oral history. It holds conferences and training courses and has a network of groups and individuals all over Britain, as well as publishing a twice-yearly journal.

International Oral History Association
Address: Almuth Leh, Treasurer, International Oral History Association, c/o Institut für Geschichte und Biographie, Fernuniversität Hagen, Leibigstr. 11, D-58511 Lüdenscheid, Germany
Email: agreen@waikato.ac.nz
Website: www.ioha.fgv.br
The association provides a forum for oral historians around the world, in order to foster international communication and cooperation and a better understanding of the nature and value of oral history.

BBC History Website
Address: The Editor, BBC History Website, Room 2476, BBC White City, 201 Wood Lane, London W12 7TS, UK
Email: via the website
Website: www.bbc.co.uk/history
The site contains audio memories and archives searchable by topic or place.

Imperial War Museum
Address: Department of Sound Records, Imperial War Museum, Lambeth Road, London SE1 6HZ, UK
Tel: 0207 416 5363
Fax: 0207 416 5379
Email: sound@iwm.org.uk

Website: www.iwm.org.uk/collections/sound.htm

The museum holds mainly oral history interviews, but also speeches, broadcasts, sound effects, lectures and poetry readings, spanning from the Boer War to the Gulf War.

National Sound Archive

Address: The Recorded Sound Information Service, The British Library Sound Archive, 96 Euston Road, London NW1 2DB, UK

Tel: 0207 412 7440

Fax: 0207 412 7441

Email: sound-archive@bl.uk

Website: http://www.bl.uk/collections/sound-archive/nsa.html

The Sound Archive holds over a million discs, 185,000 tapes, and many other sound and video recordings. The collections come from all over the world and cover the entire range of recorded sound from music, drama and literature, to oral history and wildlife sounds.

Moving Here Archive

Website: www.movinghere.org.uk

Excellent web-based archive of oral history and factual history of those who came from the British Empire and Commonwealth to live in Britain.

Archive and Museum of Black Heritage

Address: 378 Coldharbour Lane, Brixton, London SW9 8LF, UK

Tel: 0207 326 4154

Fax: 0207 738 7168

Email: info@aambh.org.uk

Website: www.aambh.org.uk

The museum runs a programme of outreach and education, cataloguing, research and exhibitions, relating to black history in Britain.

BE ME

Black and Ethnic Minority Experience Archive in Wolverhampton

Website: www.be-me.org

BE ME holds over 100 audio/video interviews that tell the historical experiences of African-Caribbean and Asian people who came to Wolverhampton after the Second World War.

Black and Asian Studies Association

Address: 28 Russell Square, London WC1B 5BS, UK

Website: www.basauk.com

Based at the Institute of Commonwealth Studies, BASA produces a regular newsletter and the website has good biographies of significant figures in antiracist history.

Black Cultural Archive
Address: 378 Coldharbour Lane, Brixton, London SW9 8LF, UK
Tel: 0207 737 2770
In association with Middlesex University, the archive has the largest specialist collection of records relating to black heritage and history in the country, with some 5,000 objects, artefacts and videotapes and 20,000 documents, which trace black life in Britain since AD 208.

Casbah
Address: c/o Institute of Commonwealth Studies, 28 Russell Square, London WC1B 5DS, UK
Tel: 0207 862 8842
Email: icommlib@sas/ac/il
Website: www.casbah.ac.uk
Holds a database of archive, printed and audio-visual resources, relating to Caribbean studies and the history of black and Asian people in the UK.

Centre for Research in Ethnic Relations
Address: University of Warwick, Coventry CV4 7AL, UK
Tel: 0247 652 4869
Fax: 0247 652 4324
Email: crer@warwick.ac.uk
Website: http://www.warwick.ac.uk/fac/soc/CRER_RC/
The CRER is the major academic body in the UK for the research and teaching of aspects of race, migration and ethnic relations.

East Midlands Oral History Archive
Address: Centre for Urban History, University of Leicester, Leicester LE1 7RH, UK
Tel: 0116 252 5065
Fax: 0116 252 5769
Email: emoha@le.ac.uk
Website: http://www.le.ac.uk/emoha/
The project's aims are to conserve and develop oral history resources in the East Midlands. It also has a substantial online catalogue.

Eastside Community Heritage
Address: The Old Town Hall, 29 The Broadway, Stratford, London E15 4BQ, UK
Tel: 0208 519 1827/ 0208 557 8609
Email: info@hidden-histories.org
Website: www.hidden-histories.org
Eastside Community Heritage documents the lives of East Londoners.

Ethnic Communities Oral History Project
Address: c/o Hammersmith and Fulham Archives, The Lilla Huset, 191 Talgarth Road, London W6 8BJ, UK

Tel: 0208 741 5159
Email: lbhfarchives@hotmail.com
Website: www.hfusc.org.uk/ecohp
The project was founded to give ordinary people a voice in historical material. It includes
Hammersmith and Fulham Ethnic Communities Oral History Project.

Museum of London
Address: London Wall, London EC2Y 5HN, UK
Tel: 0207 600 3699
Fax: 0870 444 3853
Email: info@museumoflondon.org.uk
Website: www.museum-london.org.uk/MOLsite/menu.htm
The museum holds a quarter of a million years of history, including 4,000 hours of oral
history recordings on different aspects of London life.

Northamptonshire Black History Project
Address: Carolyn Abel, Doddridge Centre, 109 St James Road, Northampton NN5 5LD, UK
Tel: 01604 590967
Email: Carolyn_abel@hotmail.com
The project aims to archive the history of Northamptonshire's black organizations and
provides a comprehensive oral history from first generation 'elders' within the community.

Picture Credits

Chapter One
Alok and Priti Ray: pp. 18, 19
Bristol Record Office: pp. 3, 4, 6, 7, 8, 9, 10
British Empire and Commonwealth
  Museum: pp. 2, 7, 8, 9, 10
Hazel Hooper: pp. x, 13, 24
HTV Film Archive: pp. 17, 23
Hulton Archive: p. 14
Norman Jones: pp. 20, 21, 22
Rosalind Balcon: p. 12
Sadie Regan: p. 16

Chapter Two
All Hazel Hooper's photographs.

Chapter Three
All Precious McKenzie's photographs except:
Bristol Evening Post: pp. 51, 52, 53, 56
HTV Film Archive: pp. 40, 49, 50
Popperfoto.com: p. 55
Testimony Films: p. 40

Chapter Four
All Rosalind Balcon's photographs except:
Elspeth Huxley collection, British Empire
  and Commonwealth Museum: p. 62
Testimony Films: p. 58

Chapter Five
All John Hennessey's photographs except:
Bristol Record Office: p. 75
Hulton Archive: p. 79
Testimony Films: pp. 74, 75

Chapter Six
All Rosa Hui's photographs except:

British Empire and Commonwealth
  Museum: pp. 86, 96
Testimony Films: p. 84

Chapter Seven
All Alice Harper's photos except:
Testimony Films: p. 98

Chapter Eight
All Alan Chidgey's photos except:
Testimony Films: p. 114

Chapter Nine
All Roy Hackett's photographs and archive
  except:
HTV Film Archive: pp. 126, 127, 128, 132,
  134–5, 136, 138–9
Testimony Films: p. 122

Chapter Ten
All Mohindra Chowdhry's photographs
  except:
Testimony Films: p. 142

Chapter Eleven
All Sheila Mitchell Bane's photographs and
  archive except:
Testimony Films: p. 152

Chapter Twelve
British Empire and Commonwealth
  Museum: pp. 172 top, 182, 184
Hazel Hooper: pp. 171 bottom, 172 bottom
HTV Film Archive: pp. 179, 181
Joe Short: pp. 174, 175, 177
Malcolm X Centre Elders' Forum: pp. 168, 180
Norman Jones: p. 171 top

Index

Page numbers in italics refer to illustrations